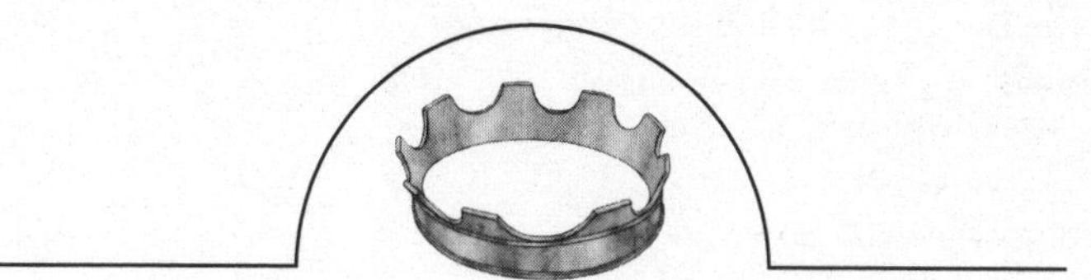

THE STORY FOR KIDS

DISCOVER THE BIBLE FROM BEGINNING TO END

SELECTIONS FROM THE NEW INTERNATIONAL READER'S VERSION

The Story for Kids, Discover the Bible from Beginning to End

Art production by Dan Davis

Published by Zonderkidz

Grand Rapids, Michigan 49530, U.S.A.

www.zonderkidz.com

Library of Congress Catalog Card Number: 2010943071

Printed in the United States of America

---

13 14 15 16 17 18 19 20 21 22 /DCI/ 18 17 16 15 14 13 12 11 10 9

You will be pleased to know that a portion of the purchase price of your new NIrV Bible has been provided to Biblica, Inc.™ to help spread the gospel of Jesus Christ around the world!

Contents

Welcome to *The Story*— God's Story

This book tells the grandest, most compelling story of all time: the story of a true God who loves his children, who established for them a way of salvation and provided a route to eternity. Each story in these 31 chapters reveals the God of grace—the God who speaks; the God who acts; the God who listens; the God whose love for his people culminated in his sacrifice of Jesus, his only Son, to atone for the sins of humanity.

What's more: this same God is alive and active today—still listening, still acting, still pouring out his grace on us. His grace extends to our daily foibles; our ups, downs, and in-betweens; our moments of questions and fears; and most important, our response to his call on our lives. He's the same God who forgave David's failures and rescued Jonah from the dark belly of a fish. This same heavenly Father who shepherded the Israelites through the wilderness desires to shepherd us through our wanderings, to help us get past our failures and rescue us for eternity.

It's our prayer that these stories will encourage you to listen for God's call on your life, as he helps write your own story.

Max Lucado and Randy Frazee

Preface

The Story for Kids is unlike any book you've ever read. Think about your favorite book. What does it have in it? Adventures? Excitement? Drama? Heroes? The book you're holding has all those things and more. But unlike many other books you may have read, this story is completely true. It's a Bible that reads like a novel.

If you've read the Bible before, you know how long it is. It has chapter and verse numbers to help you find Bible passages. Maybe you've looked up Bible verses during Sunday school.

In *The Story for Kids*, these numbers are gone, and instead selections of Bible text were put in order according to when each story happened in history. Using the New International Reader's Version (NIrV), this book has actual Bible text along with transitions written especially to help link parts of the Bible together so it's easier to understand what each story means and how they go together. The transitions are in *italic* font to show they are not part of the Bible text.

After each story, you will find discussion questions. Try talking about your answers with your family, friends, or Sunday school class. You might be surprised what they say!

We hope *The Story for Kids* helps you understand the Bible better and helps you see how the Bible relates to your life.

1

The Beginning of Life as We Know It

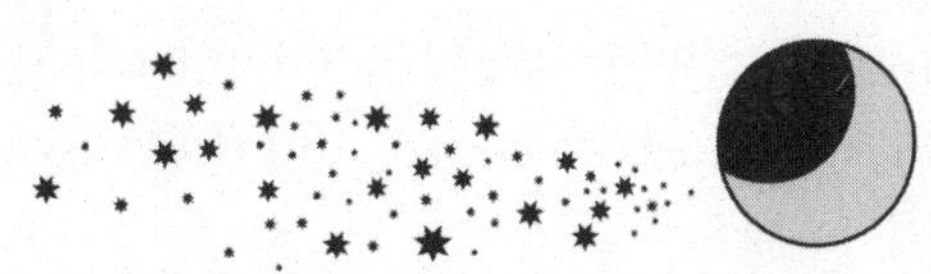

In the beginning, God created the heavens and the earth. The earth didn't have any shape. And it was empty. Darkness was over the surface of the ocean. At that time, the ocean covered the earth. The Spirit of God was hovering over the waters.

God said, "Let there be light." And there was light. God saw that the light was good. He separated the light from the darkness. God called the light "day." He called the darkness "night." There was evening, and there was morning. It was day one.

God said, "Let there be a huge space between the waters. Let it separate water from water." And that's exactly what happened. God made the huge space between the waters. He separated the water that was under the space from the water that was above it. God called the huge space "sky." There was evening, and there was morning. It was day two.

God said, "Let the water under the sky be gathered into one place. Let dry ground appear." And that's exactly what happened. God called the dry ground "land." He called the waters that were gathered together "oceans." And God saw that it was good.

Then God said, "Let the land produce plants. Let them bear their own seeds. And let there be trees on the land that bear fruit with seeds in it. Let each kind of plant or tree have its own kind of seeds." And that's exactly what happened.

And there was evening, and there was morning. It was day three.

God said, "Let there be lights in the huge space of the sky. Let them separate the day from the night. Let them serve as signs to mark off the seasons and the days and the years. Let them serve as lights in the huge space of the sky to give light on the earth." And that's exactly what happened.

God made two great lights. He made the larger light to rule over the day. He made the smaller light to rule over the night. He also made the stars.

God put the lights in the huge space of the sky to give light on the earth. He put them there to rule over the day and the night. He put them there to separate light from darkness.

God saw that it was good. And there was evening, and there was morning. It was day four.

God said, "Let the waters be filled with living things. Let birds fly above the earth across the huge space of the sky."

So God created the great creatures of the ocean. He created every living and moving thing that fills the waters. He created all kinds of them. He created every kind of bird that flies. And God saw that it was good.

God blessed them. He said, "Have little ones and increase your numbers. Fill the water in the oceans. Let there be more and more birds on the earth."

There was evening, and there was morning. It was day five.

God said, "Let the land produce all kinds of living creatures. Let there be livestock, and creatures that move along the ground, and wild animals. Let there be all kinds of them." And that's exactly what happened.

God made all kinds of wild animals. He made all kinds of livestock. He made all kinds of creatures that move along the ground. And God saw that it was good.

Then God said, "Let us make man in our likeness. Let them rule over the fish in the waters and the birds of the air. Let them rule over the livestock and over the whole earth. Let them rule over all of the creatures that move along the ground."

So God created man in his own likeness.
He created him in the likeness of God.
He created them as male and female.

God blessed them. He said to them, "Have children and increase your numbers. Fill the earth and bring it under your control. Rule over the fish in the waters and the birds of the air. Rule over every living creature that moves on the ground."

Then God said, "I am giving you every plant on the face of the whole earth that bears its own seeds. I am giving you every tree that has fruit with seeds in it. All of them will be given to you for food.

"I am giving every green plant to all of the land animals and the birds of the air for food. I am also giving the plants to all of the creatures that move on the ground. I am giving them to every living thing that breathes." And that's exactly what happened.

God saw everything he had made. And it was very good. There was evening, and there was morning. It was day six.

So the heavens and the earth and everything in them were completed.

By the seventh day God had finished the work he had been doing. So on the seventh day he rested from all of his work. God blessed the seventh day and made it holy. He rested on it. After he had created everything, he rested from all of the work he had done.

The LORD God put the man in the Garden of Eden. He put him there to work its ground and to take care of it.

The LORD God gave the man a command. He said, "You can eat the fruit of any tree that is in the garden. But you must not eat the fruit of the tree of the knowledge of good and evil. If you do, you can be sure that you will die."

The serpent was more clever than any of the wild animals the LORD God had made. The serpent said to the woman, "Did God really say, 'You must not eat the fruit of any tree that is in the garden'?"

The woman said to the serpent, "We can eat the fruit of the trees that are in the garden. But God did say, 'You must not eat the fruit of the tree that is in the middle of the garden. Do not even touch it. If you do, you will die.' "

"You can be sure that you won't die," the serpent said to the woman. "God knows that when you eat the fruit of that tree, you will know things you have never known before. You will be able to tell the difference between good and evil. You will be like God."

The woman saw that the fruit of the tree was good to eat. It was also pleasing to look at. And it would make a person wise. So she took some of the fruit and ate it. She also gave some to her husband, who was with her. And he ate it.

Then both of them knew things they had never known before. They realized they were naked. So they sewed fig leaves together and made clothes for themselves.

Then the man and his wife heard the LORD God walking in the garden. It was the coolest time of the day. They hid from the LORD God among the trees of the garden.

But the LORD God called out to the man. "Where are you?" he asked.

"I heard you in the garden," the man answered. "I was afraid. I was naked, so I hid."

The LORD God said, "Who told you that you were naked? Have you eaten the fruit of the tree I commanded you not to eat?"

The man said, "It was the woman you put here with me. She gave me some fruit from the tree. And I ate it."

Then the LORD God said to the woman, "What have you done?"

The woman said, "The serpent tricked me. That's why I ate the fruit."

So the LORD God spoke to the serpent. He said, "Because you have done this,

I am putting a curse on you.
  You are cursed more than all of the livestock and all of the wild animals.
You will crawl on the ground.
  You will eat dust all of the days of your life.
I will put hatred between you and the woman.
  Your children and her children will be enemies.
Her son will crush your head.
  And you will crush his heel."

The LORD God said to the woman,

"I will greatly increase your pain when you give birth.
    You will be in pain when you have children.
You will long for your husband.
    And he will rule over you."

The LORD God said to Adam, "You listened to your wife. You ate the fruit of the tree that I commanded you about. I said, 'You must not eat its fruit.'

So I am putting a curse on the ground because of what
        you did.
    All the days of your life you will have to work hard to
        get food from the ground.
You will eat the plants of the field,
    even though the ground produces thorns and thistles.
You will have to work hard and sweat a lot
    to produce the food you eat.
You were made out of the ground.
    And you will return to it.
You are dust.
    So you will return to it."

Adam named his wife Eve. She would become the mother of every living person.

The LORD God made clothes out of animal skins for Adam and his wife to wear. The LORD God said, "The man has become like one of us. He can now tell the difference between good and evil. He must not be allowed to reach out his hand and pick fruit from the tree of life and eat it. If he does, he will live forever."

So the LORD God drove the man out of the Garden of Eden to work the ground he had been made out of.

God put angels with a flaming sword at the entrance of the garden to keep Adam and Eve from eating the fruit from the tree of life.

As time went by, Adam and Eve had sons and daughters. Later their children had children of their own. After Adam and Eve sinned, sinning was all people could think about.

The LORD saw how bad the sins of man had become on the earth. All of the thoughts in his heart were always directed only toward what was evil. The LORD was very sad that he had made man on the earth. His heart was filled with pain.

But the LORD was pleased with Noah...

Noah was a godly man. He was without blame among the people of his time. He walked with God. Noah had three sons. Their names were Shem, Ham and Japheth.

So God said to Noah ... "Make yourself an ark out of cypress wood. Make rooms in it. Cover it with tar inside and out. Here is how I want you to build it. The ark has to be 450 feet long. It has to be 75 feet wide and 45 feet high. Make a roof for it. Leave the sides of the ark open a foot and a half from the top. Put a door in one side of the ark. Make lower, middle and upper decks.

"I am going to bring a flood on the earth. It will destroy all life under the sky. It will destroy every living creature that breathes. Everything on earth will die.

"But I will make my covenant with you. You will enter the ark. Your sons and your wife and your sons' wives will enter it with you.

"Bring two of every living thing into the ark. Bring male and female of them into it. They will be kept alive with you. Two of every kind of bird will come to you. Two of every kind of animal will come to you. And two of every kind of creature that moves along the ground will come to you. All of them will be kept alive with you.

"Take every kind of food that you will need. Store it away. It will be food for you and for them."

Noah did everything exactly as God commanded him.

Then the LORD said to Noah, "Go into the ark with your whole family."

Once Noah's family and all the animals were safe inside the ark, God closed the door. Noah was 600 years old when the flood came.

For 40 days the flood kept coming on the earth. As the waters rose higher, they lifted the ark high above the earth. The waters rose higher and higher on the earth. And the ark floated on the water.

The waters rose on the earth until all of the high mountains under the entire sky were covered. The waters continued to rise until they covered the mountains by more than 20 feet.

Every living thing that moved on the earth died. The birds, the livestock and the wild animals died. All of the creatures that fill the earth also died. And so did every human being.

Only Noah and those who were with him in the ark were left.

The waters flooded the earth for 150 days.

But God showed concern for Noah. He also showed concern for all of the wild animals and livestock that were with Noah in the ark.

So God sent a wind over the earth. And the waters began to go down. The springs at the bottom of the oceans had been closed. The windows of the skies had been closed. And the rain had stopped falling from the sky.

The water continued to go down from the earth. At the end of the 150 days the water had gone down. On the 17th day of the seventh month, the ark came to rest on the mountains of Ararat. The waters continued to go down until the tenth month. On the first day of the month, the tops of the mountains could be seen.

Noah sent out a dove to see if it was safe to come out. The dove couldn't find any place to land, so Noah took it back inside. After seven days, Noah sent the dove again. When the dove came back with a fresh leaf, Noah knew that the water was going down. He waited seven more days, and he sent the dove out a third time. This time it didn't return.

Then God said to Noah, "Come out of the ark. Bring your wife and your sons and their wives with you.

"Bring out every kind of living thing that is with you. Bring the birds, the animals, and all of the creatures that move along the ground. Then they can multiply on the earth. They can have little ones and increase their numbers."

So Noah came out of the ark. His sons and his wife and his sons' wives were with him. All of the animals came out of the ark ...

Then Noah built an altar to honor the LORD.

Then God gave his blessing to Noah and his sons. He said to them, "Have children and increase your numbers. Fill the earth.

"All of the land animals will be afraid of you. All of the birds of the air will fear you. Every creature that moves along the ground will fear you. Every fish in the oceans will also be afraid of you. Every living thing is put under your control.

"I am now making my covenant with you and with all of your children who will be born after you.

"The waters of a flood will never destroy all life again. A flood will never destroy the earth again."

God continued, "My covenant is between me and you and every living thing with you. It is a covenant for all time to come.

"Here is the sign of the covenant I am making. I have put my rainbow in the clouds. It will be the sign of the covenant between me and the earth.

"When the rainbow appears in the clouds, I will see it. I will remember that my covenant will last forever."

When the flood ended, the only people in the world were Noah and his family. Noah's sons had children and their children had children, so after a while there were thousands and thousands of people again.

Discussion Questions

1. Do you like to create things? Describe something you have made or drawn. What do you like about making or creating something?

2. Have you ever done something your mom or dad told you not to do? What happened when they found out? How did it feel when you knew they were aware of what you had done?

3. God put a rainbow in the sky as a sign of his promise to never flood the world again. Have you ever made a promise to someone? How did you show that person you were serious about keeping that promise?

2

God Builds a Nation

Abram and his wife Sarai lived in Haran. God had a plan for Abram. God wanted Abram to start a new nation. He would love and bless Abram and all his future family members. But Abram and Sarai were old, and they still didn't have any children. How could they build this nation if they had no children or grandchildren? God promised he would take care of that.

The LORD had said to Abram, "Leave your country and your people. Leave your father's family. Go to the land I will show you.

"I will make you into a great nation.
  I will bless you.
I will make your name great.
  You will be a blessing to others.

I will bless those who bless you.
I will put a curse on anyone who calls down a curse on you.
All nations on earth will be blessed because of you."

So Abram left, just as the LORD had told him. Lot went with him. Abram was 75 years old when he left Haran.

He took his wife Sarai and his nephew Lot. They took all of the things they had gotten in Haran. They also took the workers they had gotten there.

They set out for the land of Canaan. And they arrived there.

[Abram] had faith. So he obeyed God. God called him to go to a place he would later receive as his own. So he went. He did it even though he didn't know where he was going.

Lot was moving around with Abram. Lot also had flocks and herds and tents.

But the land didn't have enough food for both of them. They had large herds and many servants. So they weren't able to stay together.

The LORD spoke to Abram after Lot had left him. He said, "Look up from where you are. Look north and south. Look east and west. I will give you all of the land that you see. I will give it to you and your children after you forever.

"I will make your children like the dust of the earth. Can dust be counted? If it can, then your children can be counted. Go. Walk through the land. See how long and wide it is. I am giving it to you."

So Abram moved his tents. He went to live near the large trees of Mamre at Hebron. There he built an altar to honor the LORD.

Some time later, Abram had a vision. The LORD said to him,

"Abram, do not be afraid.
  I am like a shield to you.
  I am your very great reward."

But Abram said, "LORD and King, what can you give me? I still don't have any children. My servant Eliezer comes from Damascus. When I die, he will get everything I own." Abram continued, "You haven't given me any children. So a servant in my house will get everything I own."

Then a message came to Abram from the LORD. He said, "This man will not get what belongs to you. A son will come from your own body. He will get everything you own."

The LORD took Abram outside and said, "Look up at the sky. Count the stars, if you can." Then he said to him, "That is how many children you will have."

Abram believed the LORD. The LORD accepted Abram because he believed. So his faith made him right with the LORD.

When Abram was 99 years old, the LORD appeared to him. He said, "I am the Mighty God. Walk with me and live without any blame. I will now put into practice my covenant between me and you. I will greatly increase your numbers."

Abram fell with his face to the ground. God said to him, "As for me, this is my covenant with you. You will be the father of many nations.

"You will not be called Abram anymore. Your name will be Abraham, because I have made you a father of many nations. I will give you many children. Nations will come from you. And kings will come from you.

"I will make my covenant with you. It will last forever. It will be between me and you and your children after you for all time to come. I will be your God. And I will be the God of all of your family after you.

"You are now living in Canaan as an outsider. But I will give you the whole land of Canaan. You will own it forever. So will your children after you. And I will be their God."

God also said to Abraham, "As for Sarai your wife, do not call her Sarai anymore. Her name will be Sarah. I will give her my blessing. You can be sure that I will give you a son by

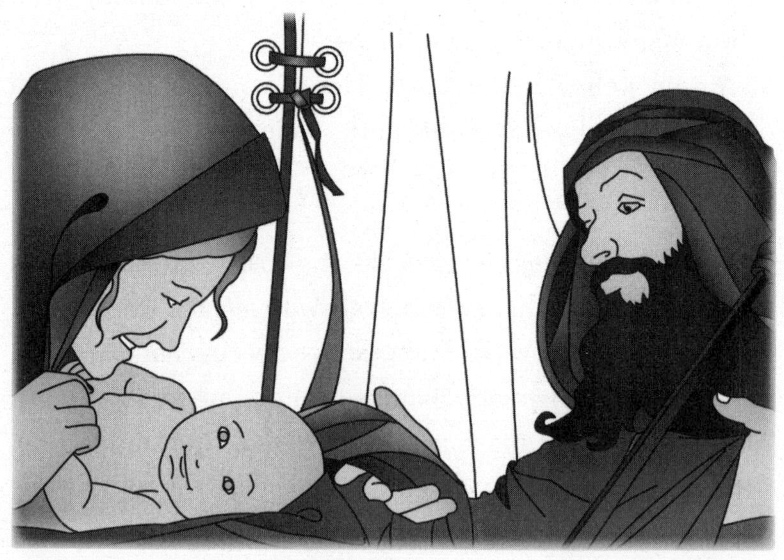

her. I will bless her so that she will be the mother of nations. Kings of nations will come from her."

The LORD was gracious to Sarah, just as he had said he would be. He did for Sarah what he had promised to do. Sarah became pregnant. She had a son by Abraham when he was old. He was born at the exact time God had promised him.

Abraham gave the name Isaac to the son Sarah had by him.

Abraham was 100 years old when his son Isaac was born to him.

Sarah said, "God has given laughter to me. Everyone who hears about this will laugh with me."

She continued, "Who would have said to Abraham that Sarah would nurse children? But I've had a son by him when he is old."

Abraham had faith. So God made it possible for him to become a father. He became a father even though he was too old. Sarah also was too old to have children. But Abraham believed that the One who made the promise was faithful.

Because Abraham trusted God even when things seemed impossible, God blessed him. Abraham was very rich. He had many sheep and cattle—and he finally had the son he had always wanted. God continued to bless Abraham's family and create a special nation.

Discussion Questions

1. Have you ever had to move away and go to a new school?

   If yes, how did it make you feel?

   If no, do you know any kids at your school or church who are new? What can you do to make them feel welcome?

2. Have you ever done something that seemed impossible at first? What did you do? What made you decide to go ahead and do the "impossible"?

3

Joseph: From Slave to Deputy Pharaoh

Abraham and Sarah's son Isaac grew up and got married. He had a son named Jacob. God blessed Jacob like he had blessed Abraham and Isaac. Jacob had twelve sons—but his favorite son was Joseph.

Joseph's brothers were jealous of him because Jacob gave Joseph a colorful robe. Joseph had unusual dreams about stars and bundles of grain bowing down to him, and he told his brothers about the dreams. When Joseph's brothers realized their younger brother thought they would one day bow down to him, they hated him even more.

[Jacob] said to Joseph, "As you know, your brothers are taking care of the flocks near Shechem. Come. I'm going to send you to them."

"All right," Joseph replied.

So [Jacob] said to him, "Go to your brothers. See how they are doing. Also see how the flocks are doing. Then come back and tell me." So he sent him away from the Hebron Valley.

[His brothers] saw him a long way off. Before he reached them, they made plans to kill him.

"Here comes that dreamer!" they said to one another. "Come. Let's kill him. Let's throw him into one of these empty wells. Let's say that a wild animal ate him up. Then we'll see whether his dreams will come true."

Reuben heard them. He tried to save Joseph from them. "Let's not take his life," he said. "Let's not spill any blood. Throw him into this empty well here in the desert. But don't harm him yourselves."

Reuben said that to save Joseph from them. He was hoping he could take him back to his father.

When Joseph came to his brothers, he was wearing his beautiful robe. They took it away from him. And they threw him into the well. The well was empty. There wasn't any water in it.

Then they sat down to eat their meal. As they did, they saw some Ishmaelite traders coming from Gilead. Their camels were loaded with spices, lotion and myrrh. They were on their way to take them down to Egypt.

Judah said to his brothers, "What will we gain if we kill our brother and try to cover up what we've done? Come. Let's sell him to these traders. Let's not harm him ourselves. After all, he's our brother. He's our own flesh and blood." Judah's brothers agreed with him.

The traders from Midian came by. Joseph's brothers pulled him up out of the well. They sold him to the Ishmaelite traders for eight ounces of silver. Then the traders took him to Egypt.

Then they got Joseph's beautiful robe. They killed a goat and dipped the robe in the blood. They took it back to their father. They said, "We found this. Take a look at it. See if it's your son's robe."

Jacob recognized it. He said, "It's my son's robe! A wild animal has eaten him up. Joseph must have been torn to pieces."

Jacob tore his clothes. He put on black clothes. Then he sobbed over his son for many days.

All of Jacob's other sons and daughters came to comfort him. But they weren't able to. He said, "I'll be full of sorrow when I go down into the grave to be with my son." So Joseph's father sobbed over him.

Joseph had been taken down to Egypt. An Egyptian named Potiphar had bought him from the Ishmaelite traders who had taken him there. Potiphar was one of Pharaoh's officials. He was the captain of the palace guard.

The LORD was with Joseph. He gave him great success. Joseph lived in Potiphar's house.

Joseph's master saw that the LORD was with him. He saw that the LORD gave Joseph success in everything he did. So Potiphar was pleased with Joseph. He made him his attendant. He put Joseph in charge of his house. He told Joseph to take good care of everything he owned.

From that time on, the LORD blessed Potiphar's family and

servants because of Joseph. He blessed everything Potiphar had in his house and field.

So Potiphar told Joseph to take good care of everything he owned. With Joseph in charge, he didn't have to worry about anything except the food he ate.

Potiphar's wife thought Joseph was handsome, and she wanted to spend time with him. Joseph knew that he should stay away from her because she was Potiphar's wife. He didn't want to do anything wrong or make Potiphar mad at him. But Potiphar's wife really liked Joseph. When she tried to get romantic with him one day, Joseph ran away from her, but he accidentally left his coat behind. When Potiphar came home, his wife lied and said Joseph tried to attack her.

When Joseph's master heard her story, he became very angry. So he put Joseph in prison. It was the place where the king's prisoners were kept.

While Joseph was there in the prison, the LORD was with him. He was kind to him.

So the man who was running the prison was pleased with Joseph. He put Joseph in charge of all of the prisoners. He made him accountable for everything that was done there. The man who ran the prison didn't pay attention to anything that was in Joseph's care.

The LORD was with Joseph. He gave Joseph success in everything he did.

Joseph could explain what any dream meant because God gave him the answers. While Joseph was in prison, God used dreams to help Joseph. Pharaoh was mad at his baker and his wine-taster, and he threw them in jail. One night they both had strange dreams, so they asked Joseph what the dreams meant. Joseph told them, and their dreams came true. The wine-taster got out of jail. Two years went by. One day the wine-taster heard that Pharaoh was having some strange dreams. The wine-taster remembered Joseph, and he told Pharaoh that Joseph might be able to tell him what his dreams meant.

In the morning [Pharoah] was worried. So he sent for all of the magicians and wise men of Egypt. Pharaoh told them his dreams. But no one could tell him what they meant.

So Pharaoh sent for Joseph. He was quickly brought out of the prison. Joseph shaved himself and changed his clothes. Then he came to Pharaoh.

Pharaoh said to Joseph, "I had a dream. No one can tell me what it means. But I've heard that when you hear a dream you can explain it."

"I can't do it," Joseph replied to Pharaoh. "But God will give Pharaoh the answer he wants."

Pharaoh dreamt that seven fat cows were eaten by seven skinny cows, and seven big wheat stalks were eaten by seven thin ones. When he told Joseph about these dreams, Joseph told him what the dreams meant. There would be seven years of big harvests and a lot of food, and then there would be seven years when no food would grow. God also told Joseph that Pharaoh had to save food from the seven good years so no one would starve later.

The plan seemed good to Pharaoh and all of his officials. So Pharaoh said to them, "The spirit of God is in this man. We can't find anyone else like him, can we?"

Then Pharaoh said to Joseph, "God has made all of this known to you. No one is as wise and understanding as you are. You will be in charge of my palace. All of my people must obey your orders. I will be greater than you only because I'm the one who sits on the throne."

So Pharaoh said to Joseph, "I'm putting you in charge of the whole land of Egypt."

Then Pharaoh took his ring off his finger. It was the ring he used to stamp all of the official papers. He put it on Joseph's finger. He dressed him in robes that were made out of fine linen. He put a gold chain around his neck.

He also had him ride in a chariot. Joseph was now next in command after Pharaoh. People went in front of him and shouted, "Get down on your knees!"

By doing all of those things, Pharaoh put Joseph in charge of the whole land of Egypt.

Then Pharaoh said to Joseph, "I am Pharaoh. But without your word, no one will do anything in the whole land of Egypt."

Seven good years yielded plenty of food, and everyone was happy. But when the seven bad years came, people from many countries—including Jacob and his sons—didn't have any food. So they went to Egypt to buy food there. When Jacob's sons arrived in Egypt, they saw Joseph, but they didn't recognize him. But Joseph knew they were his brothers, and he wanted to see if they were sorry for selling him as a slave.

Joseph tested his brothers by scaring them and making them think they were in trouble for stealing. But he always made sure they received plenty of food and didn't pay for it, because he still loved his brothers. Knowing Joseph was a great ruler of Egypt, Joseph's brothers bowed down to him in his presence—just like in Joseph's star and bundles of grain dreams! Finally, Joseph made an announcement.

Joseph said to his brothers, "Come close to me." So they did.

Then he said, "I am your brother Joseph. I'm the one you sold into Egypt. But don't be upset. And don't be angry with yourselves because you sold me here. God sent me ahead of you to save many lives.

"For two years now, there hasn't been enough food in the land. And for the next five years, people won't be plowing or gathering crops. But God sent me ahead of you to keep some of you alive on earth. He sent me here to save your lives by an act of mighty power.

"So then, it wasn't you who sent me here. It was God. He made me like a father to Pharaoh. He made me master of Pharaoh's whole house. He made me ruler of the whole land of Egypt.

"Tell my father about all of the honor that has been given to me in Egypt. Tell him about everything you have seen. And bring my father down here quickly."

So they went up out of Egypt. They came to their father Jacob in the land of Canaan. They told him, "Joseph is still alive! In fact, he is ruler of the whole land of Egypt."

Jacob was shocked. He didn't believe them. So they told him everything Joseph had said to them.

Jacob saw the carts Joseph had sent to carry him back. That gave new life to their father Jacob. [He] said, "I believe it now! My son Joseph is still alive. I'll go and see him before I die."

Jacob sent Judah ahead of him to Joseph. He sent him to get directions to Goshen. And so they arrived in the area of Goshen.

Then Joseph had his servants get his chariot ready. He went to Goshen to meet his father Israel. As soon as he came to his father, Joseph threw his arms around him. Then Joseph sobbed for a long time.

So Joseph settled his father and his brothers in Egypt. He gave them property in the best part of the land, just as Pharaoh had directed him to do.

Discussion Questions

1. If you have siblings, what sorts of activities do you like doing together? Choose one and explain why you enjoy that activity.
2. Have you ever lied to your mom or dad? Why did you lie? What happened when they found out the truth?
3. Have you ever spent the night at a friend's house and been scared because you were away from home? What did you do?

4

Out of Egypt

Jacob and Joseph died. Many years went by. Soon, there were thousands and thousands of Hebrews living in Egypt.

Then a new king came to power in Egypt. He didn't know anything about Joseph.

"Look," he said to his people. "The Israelites are far too many for us. Come. We must deal with them carefully. If we don't, they will increase their numbers even more. Then if war breaks out, they'll join our enemies. They'll fight against us and leave the country."

So the Egyptians put slave drivers over the people of Israel. The slave drivers beat them down and made them work hard.

Then Pharaoh gave an order to all of his people. He said, "You must throw every baby boy into the Nile River. But let every baby girl live."

A man and a woman from the tribe of Levi got married. She became pregnant and had a son by him. She saw that her baby was a fine child. So she hid him for three months.

After that, she couldn't hide him any longer. So she got a basket that was made out of the stems of tall grass. She coated it with tar. Then she placed the child in it. She put the basket in the tall grass that grew along the bank of the Nile River. The child's sister wasn't very far away. She wanted to see what would happen to him.

Pharaoh's daughter went down to the Nile River to take a bath. Her attendants were walking along the bank of the river. She saw the basket in the tall grass. So she sent her female slave to get it.

When she opened it, she saw the baby. He was crying. She felt sorry for him. "This is one of the Hebrew babies," she said.

Then his sister spoke to Pharaoh's daughter. She asked, "Do you want me to go and get one of the Hebrew women? She could nurse the baby for you."

"Yes. Go," she answered. So the girl went and got the baby's mother.

Pharaoh's daughter said to her, "Take this baby. Nurse him for me. I'll pay you." So the woman took the baby and nursed him.

When the child grew older, she took him to Pharaoh's daughter. And he became her son. She named him Moses. She said, "I pulled him out of the water."

Moses grew up. One day, he went out to where his own people were. He watched them while they were hard at work.

He saw an Egyptian hitting a Hebrew man. The man was one of Moses' own people. Moses looked around and didn't see anyone. So he killed the Egyptian. Then he hid his body in the sand.

Moses was afraid people knew what he had done, so he left Egypt. He went to Midian, where he met a family of shepherds. He got married and became a shepherd too.

Moses was taking care of the flock of his father-in-law Jethro. Jethro was the priest of Midian. Moses led the flock to the western side of the desert. He came to Horeb. It was the mountain of God.

There the angel of the LORD appeared to him from inside a burning bush. Moses saw that the bush was on fire. But it didn't burn up. So Moses thought, "I'll go over and see this strange sight. Why doesn't the bush burn up?"

The LORD saw that Moses had gone over to look. So God spoke to him from inside the bush. He called out, "Moses! Moses!"

"Here I am," Moses said.

"Do not come any closer," God said. "Take off your sandals. The place you are standing on is holy ground." He continued, "I am the God of your father. I am the God of Abraham. I am the God of Isaac. And I am the God of Jacob."

When Moses heard that, he turned his face away. He was afraid to look at God.

The LORD said, "I have seen my people suffer in Egypt. I have heard them cry out because of their slave drivers. I am concerned about their suffering.

"So I have come down to save them from the Egyptians. I will bring them up out of that land. I will bring them into a good land. It has a lot of room. It is a land that has plenty of milk and honey.

"And now Israel's cry for help has reached me. I have seen the way the Egyptians are beating them down. So now, go. I am sending you to Pharaoh. I want you to bring the Israelites out of Egypt. They are my people."

But Moses spoke to God. "Who am I that I should go to Pharaoh?" he said. "Who am I that I should bring the Israelites out of Egypt?"

God said, "I will be with you. I will give you a miraculous sign. It will prove that I have sent you. When you have brought the people out of Egypt, all of you will worship me on this mountain."

Moses spoke to the LORD. He said, "Lord, I've never been a good speaker. And I haven't gotten any better since you spoke to me. I don't speak very well at all."

The LORD said to him, "Who makes a man able to talk? Who makes him unable to hear or speak? Who makes him able to see? Who makes him blind? It is I, the LORD. Now go. I will help you speak. I will teach you what to say."

But Moses said, "Lord, please send someone else to do it."

Then the LORD's anger burned against Moses. He said, "What about your brother, Aaron the Levite? I know he can speak well. He is already on his way to meet you. He will be glad to see you. Speak to him. Put your words in his mouth. Tell him what to say. I will help both of you speak. I will teach you what to do. He will speak to the people for you. He will be like your mouth. And you will be like God to him.

"But take this wooden staff in your hand. You will be able to do miraculous signs with it."

Moses and Aaron went to Pharaoh's palace and asked him to let the Hebrews go. But Pharaoh didn't want to let the slaves go. In fact, he was so angry that Moses and Aaron even dared to ask him to release the slaves that he decided to punish the Hebrews and make them work even harder.

Then the LORD said to Moses, "Pharaoh's heart is very stubborn. He refuses to let the people go. In the morning Pharaoh will go down to the water. Go and wait on the bank of the Nile River to meet him. Take in your hand the wooden staff that turned into a snake.

"Say to Pharaoh, 'The LORD, the God of the Hebrews, has sent me to you. He says, "Let my people go. Then they will be able to worship me in the desert. But up to now you have not listened."

" 'The LORD says, "Here is how you will know that I am the LORD. I will strike the water of the Nile River with the staff that is in my hand. The river will turn into blood. The fish in the river will die. The river will stink. The Egyptians will not be able to drink its water." ' "

The LORD said to Moses, "Tell Aaron, 'Get your staff. Reach your hand out over the waters of Egypt. The streams, waterways, ponds and all of the lakes will turn into blood. There will be blood everywhere in Egypt. It will even be in the wooden buckets and stone jars.' "

Moses and Aaron did exactly as the LORD had commanded them. Aaron held out his staff in front of Pharaoh and his officials. He struck the water of the Nile River. And all of the water turned into blood.

The fish in the Nile died. The river smelled so bad the Egyptians couldn't drink its water. There was blood everywhere in Egypt.

But the Egyptian magicians did the same things by doing their magic tricks. So Pharaoh's heart became stubborn. He wouldn't listen to Moses and Aaron, just as the LORD had said. Even that miracle didn't change Pharaoh's mind. In fact, he turned around and went into his palace.

All of the Egyptians dug holes near the Nile River to get drinking water. They couldn't drink water from the river.

Even though God turned all the water to blood, Pharaoh wouldn't let the Israelites go. So God sent frogs to cover the land, but Pharaoh still wouldn't let the Israelites go. When God sent more punishments (plagues) of gnats, flies, animal diseases, sores called boils, hail, locusts, and darkness, Pharaoh still wouldn't let the Israelites leave. He wanted to keep the Israelites as slaves. No matter what Moses said or God did, Pharaoh was determined to say no.

The LORD had spoken to Moses. He had said, "I will bring one more plague on Pharaoh and on Egypt. After that, he will let you and your people go. When he does, he will drive you completely away."

God sent one last plague and it was the worst one of all. God was going to take away the oldest son from every

Egyptian family. He told Moses to have the Israelites smear lambs' blood over their doors, so that this awful plague wouldn't happen to them. That night, all through Egypt, mothers and fathers cried as they discovered their oldest son had died. The plague killed Pharaoh's son too.

During the night, Pharaoh sent for Moses and Aaron. He said to them, "Get out of here! You and the Israelites, leave my people! Go. Worship the LORD, just as you have asked. Go. Take your flocks and herds, just as you have said. And also give me your blessing."

The people of Israel lived in Egypt for 430 years. At the end of the 430 years, to the very day, all of the LORD's people marched out of Egypt like an army.

By day the LORD went ahead of them in a pillar of cloud. It guided them on their way. At night he led them with a pillar of fire. It gave them light. So they could travel by day or at night. The pillar of cloud didn't leave its place in front of the people during the day. And the pillar of fire didn't leave its place at night.

God knew Pharaoh would soon change his mind and try to get his slaves, the Israelites, back. So God told Moses to have the Israelites walk back toward Egypt and then camp at a special place near the Red Sea. God had a plan. He wanted to lure Pharaoh into a trap.

"Pharaoh will think, 'The people of Israel are wandering around the land. They don't know which way to go. The desert is all around them.'

"I will make Pharaoh's heart stubborn. He will chase them. But I will gain glory for myself because of what will happen to Pharaoh and his whole army. And the Egyptians will know that I am the LORD." So the Israelites camped by the Red Sea.

The king of Egypt was told that the people had gotten away. Then Pharaoh and his officials changed their minds about them. They said, "What have we done? We've let the people of Israel go! We've lost our slaves and all of the work they used to do for us!"

So he had his chariot made ready. He took his army with him.

The LORD made the heart of Pharaoh, the king of Egypt, stubborn. So he chased the Israelites, who were marching out boldly. The Egyptians went after the Israelites. All of Pharaoh's horses and chariots and horsemen and troops went after them. They caught up with them as they camped by the sea.

As Pharaoh approached, the people of Israel looked up. There were the Egyptians marching after them! The Israelites were terrified. They cried out to the LORD.

They said to Moses, "Why did you bring us to the desert to die? Weren't there any graves in Egypt? What have you done to us by bringing us out of Egypt? We told you in Egypt, 'Leave us alone. Let us serve the Egyptians.' It would have been better for us to serve the Egyptians than to die here in the desert!"

Moses answered the people. He said, "Don't be afraid. Stand firm. You will see how the LORD will save you today. Do you see those Egyptians? You will never see them again. The LORD will fight for you. Just be still."

Then the LORD spoke to Moses. He said, "Why are you crying out to me? Tell the people of Israel to move on. Hold your wooden staff out. Reach your hand out over the Red Sea to part the water. Then the people can go through the sea on dry ground.

"I will make the hearts of the Egyptians stubborn. They will go in after the Israelites. I will gain glory for myself because of what will happen to Pharaoh, his whole army, his chariots and his horsemen.

"The Egyptians will know that I am the LORD. I will gain glory because of what will happen to all of them."

The angel of God had been traveling in front of Israel's army. Now he moved back and went behind them. The pillar of cloud also moved away from in front of them. Now it stood behind them. It came between the armies of Egypt and Israel. All through the night the cloud brought darkness to one side and light to the other. Neither army went near the other all night long.

Then Moses reached his hand out over the Red Sea. All that night the LORD pushed the sea back with a strong east wind. He turned the sea into dry land. The waters were parted. The people of Israel went through the sea on dry ground. There was a wall of water on their right side and on their left.

The Egyptians chased them. All of Pharaoh's horses and chariots and horsemen followed them into the sea.

Near the end of the night the LORD looked down from the pillar of fire and cloud. He saw the Egyptian army and threw it into a panic. He kept their chariot wheels from turning freely. That made the chariots hard to drive.

The Egyptians said, "Let's get away from the Israelites! The LORD is fighting for Israel against Egypt."

Then the LORD spoke to Moses. He said, "Reach your hand out over the sea. The waters will flow back over the Egyptians and their chariots and horsemen." So Moses reached

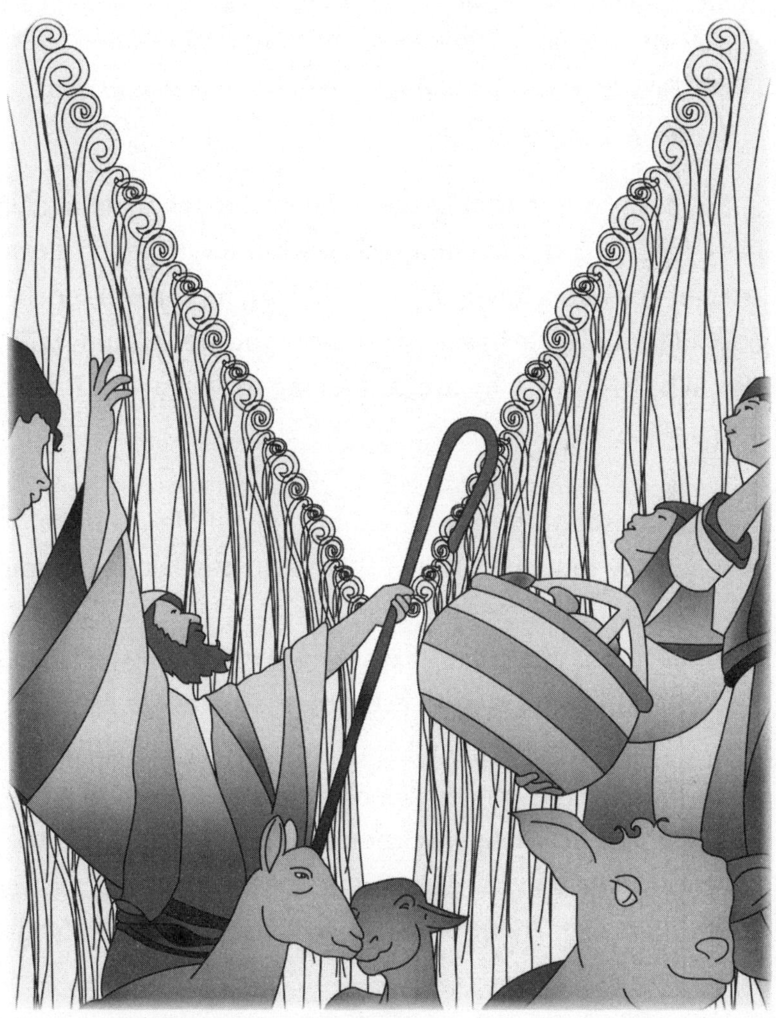

his hand out over the sea. At sunrise the sea went back to its place. The Egyptians tried to run away from the sea. But the LORD swept them into it. The water flowed back and covered the chariots and horsemen. It covered the entire army of Pharaoh that had followed the people of Israel into the sea. Not one of the Egyptians was left.

Moses led the people away from the Red Sea. Since the Israelites were really free from Egypt, they headed toward Canaan, the land God had promised them. But the Israelites weren't happy marching all day, and they started to complain.

So Moses and Aaron spoke to all of the people of Israel. They said, "In the evening you will know that the LORD brought you out of Egypt. And in the morning you will see the glory of the LORD. He has heard you say you aren't happy with him. Who are we? Why are you telling us you aren't happy with us?"

Then Moses told Aaron, "Talk to the whole community of Israel. Say to them, 'Come to the LORD. He has heard you speak against him.' "

While Aaron was talking to the whole community of Israel, they looked toward the desert. There was the glory of the LORD appearing in the cloud!

The LORD said to Moses, "I have heard the people of Israel talking about how unhappy they are. Tell them, 'When the sun goes down, you will eat meat. In the morning you will be filled with bread. Then you will know that I am the LORD your God.' "

That evening quail came and covered the camp. In the morning the ground around the camp was covered with dew. When the dew was gone, thin flakes appeared on the desert floor. They looked like frost on the ground. The people of Israel saw the flakes. They asked each other, "What's that?" They didn't know what it was.

Moses said to them, "It's the bread the LORD has given you to eat. Here is what the LORD has commanded. He has said, 'Each one of you should gather as much as you need. Take two quarts for each person who lives in your tent.'"

The people of Israel did as they were told. Some gathered a lot, and some gathered a little. When they measured it out, those who gathered a lot didn't have too much. And those who gathered a little had enough. All of them gathered only what they needed.

Discussion Questions

1. Do you pray to God before you take a test or when you try something new? If so, what do you talk to him about?

2. What are some wonderful things that have happened in your life? Did you thank God for them? Besides expressing your thanks in prayer, how else can you show God your appreciation?

3. Have you ever wondered if God was going to help you when you were afraid? What can you do when you feel this way?

5

New Rules

Moses talked with God on Mount Sinai while the Israelites were in the desert. God gave Moses ten rules—or commandments—that the Israelites had to follow as God's holy people. God wrote the ten rules on two big stone tablets. Moses took these tablets to the people, and here's what God had written:

"I am the Lord your God. I brought you out of Egypt. That is the land where you were slaves.

"Do not put any other gods in place of me.

"Do not make statues of gods that look like anything in the sky or on the earth or in the waters. Do not bow down to them or worship them. I, the Lord your God, am a jealous God. I punish the children for the sin of their parents. I punish the grandchildren and great-grandchildren of those who hate me. But for all time to come I show love to all those who love me and keep my commandments.

"Do not misuse the name of the LORD your God. The LORD will find guilty anyone who misuses his name.

"Remember to keep the Sabbath day holy. Do all of your work in six days. But the seventh day is a Sabbath in honor of the LORD your God. Do not do any work on that day... In six days I made the heavens and the earth. I made the oceans and everything in them. But I rested on the seventh day. So I blessed the Sabbath day and made it holy.

"Honor your father and mother. Then you will live a long time in the land the LORD your God is giving you.

"Do not commit murder.

"Do not commit adultery.

"Do not steal.

"Do not give false witness against your neighbor.

"Do not long for anything that belongs to your neighbor."

Moses went and told the people all of the LORD's words and laws. They answered with one voice. They said, "We will do everything the LORD has told us to do."

The LORD said to Moses, "Tell the people of Israel to bring me an offering. You must receive the offering for me from all whose hearts move them to give.

"Have them make a sacred tent for me. I will live among them. Make the holy tent and everything that belongs to it. Make them exactly like the pattern I will show you.

So God gave Moses instructions for building the ark of the covenant. The ark was a sign of God's presence, and it was holy. God told Moses to carve the ark out of wood, cover it with gold, and put two angels on the top. Only the priests could carry the ark on special poles; no one else was allowed to touch it. The ark contained a jar of manna and the two stone tablets to remind the people of how God helped them in the desert.

God also gave Moses laws for the Israelites on how to stay clean, what to eat, and when to offer sacrifices to God. The animal sacrifices paid for the person's sin. If they were sorry and gave their best animals, they were forgiven.

God gave all these instructions and laws to make sure his people stayed special. And he continued to lead and protect them as they approached the promised land.

Discussion Questions

1. What rules do you have to follow at home? (Describe three.)
2. If you break these rules, what happens?
3. Do you have a special place where you like to pray to God? If so, where is it and why is it so special to you?

6

Wandering

Every time the Israelites camped in a new place, Moses set up a special tent, called the Tent of Meeting, where God would come to talk to him. The Israelites would go to the tent and ask Moses what God wanted them to do.

While the Israelites were camping close to the promised land, God had a very exciting message for Moses. Here's what happened:

The LORD spoke to Moses. He said, "Send some men to check out the land of Canaan. I am giving it to the people of Israel. Send one leader from each of Israel's tribes."

So Moses sent them out.

[He said] "See what the land is like. See whether the people who live there are strong or weak. See whether they are few or many.

"What kind of land do they live in? Is it good or bad? What kind of towns do they live in? Do the towns have high walls around them or not? How is the soil? Is it rich land or poor land? Are there trees on it or not? Do your best to bring back some of the fruit of the land." It was the season for the first ripe grapes.

So the men went up and checked out the land.

The men came to the Valley of Eshcol. There they cut off a branch that had a single bunch of grapes on it. Two of them carried it on a pole between them. They carried some pomegranates and figs along with it.

At the end of 40 days, the men returned from checking out the land.

The men came back to Moses, Aaron and the whole community of Israel ... There the men reported to Moses and Aaron and all of the people. They showed them the fruit of the land.

They gave Moses their report. They said, "We went into the land you sent us to. It really does have plenty of milk and honey! Here's some fruit from the land.

"But the people who live there are powerful. Their cities have high walls around them and are very large."

Then Caleb interrupted the men who were speaking to Moses. He said, "We should go up and take the land. We can certainly do it."

But the men who had gone up with him spoke. They said, "We can't attack those people. They are stronger than we are." The men spread a bad report about the land among the people of Israel. They said, "The land we checked out destroys those who live in it. All of the people we saw there are very big and tall … We seemed like grasshoppers in our own eyes. And that's also how we seemed to them."

That night all of the people in the community raised their voices. They sobbed out loud.

The people of Israel spoke against Moses and Aaron. The whole community said to them, "We wish we had died in Egypt or even in this desert. Why is the LORD bringing us to this land? We're going to be killed with swords. Our enemies will capture our wives and children. Wouldn't it be better for us to go back to Egypt?"

They said to one another, "We should choose another leader. We should go back to Egypt."

Then Moses and Aaron fell with their faces to the ground. They did it in front of the whole community of Israel that was gathered there.

[Joshua and Caleb] spoke to the whole community of Israel. They said, "We passed through the land and checked it out. It's very good. If the LORD is pleased with us, he'll lead us into that land. It's a land that has plenty of milk and honey. He'll give it to us.

"But don't refuse to obey him. And don't be afraid of the people of the land. We will swallow them up. The LORD is with us. So nothing can save them. Don't be afraid of them."

The people listened to the complaining spies instead of trusting God to protect them and give them the land he had promised. God was very, very angry. God decided to punish them for doubting he could defeat the people in Canaan. He said only Joshua and Caleb would enter the promised land. All the other adults wouldn't get to live there, but their children would. So for forty years, as punishment for not trusting God, the Israelites had to wander around in the desert.

The people didn't have any water. So they gathered together to oppose Moses and Aaron. They argued with Moses. They said, "We wish we had died when our people fell dead in front of the LORD.

"Why did you bring the LORD's people into this desert? We and our livestock will die here. Why did you bring us up out of Egypt? Why did you bring us to this terrible place? It doesn't have any grain or figs. It doesn't have any grapes or pomegranates. There isn't even any water for us to drink!"

Moses and Aaron left the people. They went to the entrance to the Tent of Meeting. There they fell with their faces to the ground.

Then the glory of the LORD appeared to them. The LORD spoke to Moses. He said, "Get your wooden staff. You and your brother Aaron gather the people together. Then speak to that rock while everyone is watching. It will pour out its water. You will bring water out of the rock for the community. Then they and their livestock can drink it."

So Moses took the wooden staff from the tent. He did just as the LORD had commanded him. He and Aaron gathered the people together in front of the rock. Moses said to them, "Listen, you who refuse to obey! Do we have to bring water out of this rock for you?"

Then Moses raised his arm. He hit the rock twice with his staff. Water poured out. And the people and their livestock drank it.

But the LORD spoke to Moses and Aaron. He said, "You did not trust in me enough to honor me. You did not honor me as the holy God in front of the people of Israel. So you will not bring this community into the land I am giving them."

The Israelites continued to wander in the desert. They complained about the food, they challenged their leaders, they begged for water, they faced poisonous snakes, and

they fought battles with kings. Every time something happened, God saved his people. He used the forty years in the desert to teach the Israelites to trust him and follow his rules. The Israelites promised to obey God, and they trusted him instead of complaining. The people were almost ready to enter the promised land.

But before they entered Canaan, Moses died. The Israelites were very sad to lose their leader. God buried Moses himself.

Since then, Israel has never had a prophet like Moses. The LORD knew him face to face. Moses did many miraculous signs and wonders. The LORD had sent him to do them in Egypt. Moses did them against Pharaoh, against all of his officials and against his whole land. No one has ever had the mighty power Moses had. No one has ever done the wonderful acts he did in the sight of all of the people of Israel.

Discussion Questions

1. Do you have a place where you like to explore or ride your bike? If so, where is it or where do you go? What makes this place special to you?
2. When was the last time you got something that you wanted really badly? What was that something? What made you want it so much? Did you thank God for it?

7

The Battle Begins

Joshua was Moses' helper. The LORD said to Joshua, "My servant Moses is dead. Now then, I want you and all of these people to get ready to go across the Jordan River. I want all of you to go into the land I am about to give to the people of Israel.

"I will give all of you every place you walk on, just as I promised Moses.

"Joshua, no one will be able to stand up against you as long as you live. I will be with you, just as I was with Moses. I will never leave you. I will never desert you.

"Be strong and brave. You will lead these people, and they will take the land as their very own. It is the land I promised with an oath to give their people long ago.

"Be strong and very brave. Make sure you obey the whole law my servant Moses gave you. Do not turn away from it to the right or the left. Then you will have success everywhere you go.

So Joshua gave orders to the officers of the people. He said, "Go through the camp. Tell the people, 'Get your supplies ready. Three days from now you will go across the Jordan River right here. You will go in and take over the land. The LORD your God is giving it to you as your very own.' "

Joshua remembered that the people in Canaan were very strong. He sent spies into Jericho, one of the towns in Canaan that God wanted the Israelites to take over. When the spies got to Jericho, they met a woman named Rahab. She knew about God and his plan, and she decided to keep the spies safe.

The king of Jericho was told, "Look! Some of the people of Israel have come here tonight. They've come to check out the land."

So the king sent a message to Rahab. It said, "Bring out the men who came into your house. They've come to check out the whole land."

But the woman had hidden the two men. She said, "It's true that the men came here. But I didn't know where they had come from. They left at sunset, when it was time to close the city gate. I don't know which way they went. Go after them quickly. You might catch up with them."

But in fact she had taken them up on the roof. There she had hidden them under some flax she had piled up.

The king's men left to hunt down the spies. They took the road that leads to where the Jordan River can be crossed. As soon as they had gone out of the city, the gate was shut.

Rahab went up on the roof before the spies settled down for the night. She said to them, "I know that the LORD has given this land to you. We are very much afraid of you. Everyone who lives in this country is weak with fear because of you.

"We've heard how the LORD dried up the Red Sea for you when you came out of Egypt ...

"Because of you, we aren't brave anymore. The LORD your God is the God who rules over heaven above and earth below.

"Now then, please take an oath. Promise me in the name of the LORD that you will be kind to my family. I've been kind to you. Promise me that you will spare the lives of my father and mother. Spare my brothers and sisters. Also spare everyone in their families. Promise that you won't put any of us to death."

So the men made a promise to her. "We'll give up our lives to save yours," they said. "But don't tell anyone what we're doing. Then we'll be kind and faithful to you when the LORD gives us the land."

The house Rahab lived in was part of the city wall. So she let the spies down by a rope through the window. She had said to them, "Go up into the hills. The men who are chasing you won't be able to find you. Hide yourselves there for three days until they return. Then you can go on your way."

When the spies left, they went up into the hills. They stayed there for three days. By that time the men who were chasing them had searched all along the road. They couldn't find them. So they returned.

Then the two spies started back. They went down out of the hills. They went across the Jordan River. They came to Joshua, the son of Nun. They told him everything that had happened to them.

Joshua liked the spies' report—he knew it meant God would take care of the people once they started fighting in Canaan. Joshua had all the Israelites prepare for what God would do, and they got ready to attack Jericho. God told Joshua his plan for capturing the city. This is what happened when the Israelites came to the city of Jericho and the gates were shut tight:

Joshua had given an order to the fighting men. He had said, "Don't give a war cry. Don't raise your voices. Don't say a word until the day I tell you to shout. Then shout!"

So he had the ark of the LORD carried around the city once. Then the men returned to camp. They spent the night there.

Joshua got up early the next morning. The priests went and got the ark of the LORD. The seven priests who were carrying the seven trumpets started out. They marched in front of the ark of the LORD. They blew the trumpets. Some of the fighting men marched ahead of them. The others followed behind the ark and guarded all of them. The priests kept blowing the trumpets.

On the second day they marched around the city once. Then the men returned to camp. They did all of those things for six days.

On the seventh day, they got up at sunrise. They marched around the city, just as they had done before. But on that day they went around it seven times.

On the seventh time around, the priests blew a long blast on the trumpets.

Then Joshua gave a command to the men. He said, "Shout! The LORD has given you the city!"

The priests blew the trumpets. As soon as the fighting men heard the sound, they gave a loud shout. Then the wall fell down. Every man charged straight in. So they took the city.

The young men who had checked out the land went into Rahab's house. They brought her out along with her parents and brothers. They brought out everyone else who was there

with her. They put them in a place that was outside the camp of Israel.

Then they burned the whole city and everything that was in it. But they added the silver and gold to the treasures that were kept in the LORD's house. They also put there the articles that were made out of bronze and iron.

So the LORD was with Joshua. And Joshua became famous everywhere in the land.

After the Israelites attacked Jericho, they continued to fight. With God's help they captured many cities for the Israelites to live in someday. Joshua and his soldiers got rid of the sinful kings and people who lived in Canaan. Joshua gave the captured land and cities to each of the twelve tribes of Israel so the people had a place to live. The Israelites were finally living in the promised land!

Discussion Questions

1. Do you ever feel like everyone is picking on you? What can you do when that happens?
2. When was the last time you helped someone? What did you help them with? Do you think it is important to get something in return when you help others?
3. When you thank God for everything he has given you, what do you say or do? (Sing? Jump around? Shout for joy?)

8

A Few Good Men … and Women

The people served the LORD as long as Joshua lived. They also served him as long as the elders lived. Those were the elders who lived longer than Joshua did. They had seen all of the great things the LORD had done for Israel.

Joshua, the servant of the LORD, died. He was the son of Nun. He was 110 years old when he died.

All of the people of Joshua's time joined the members of their families who had already died. Then those who were born after them grew up. They didn't know the LORD. They didn't know what he had done for Israel.

The people of Israel did what was evil in the sight of the LORD. They served the gods that were named after Baal. They deserted the LORD, the God of their people. He had brought them out of Egypt. But now the people of Israel followed other gods and worshiped them. They served the gods of the nations that were around them. They made the LORD angry because they deserted him. They served Baal. They also served the goddesses that were named after Ashtoreth.

God sent enemies to punish the Israelites. When they cried for help, God gave them a leader, called a judge, to save and protect them from the enemy. Israel had many judges including Ehud, Deborah, Gideon, and Samson. Samson was like Israel's personal superhero—God made him really strong. No one could beat Samson, especially the Philistines. The Philistines wanted to know Samson's weakness. And they found out what it was when Samson got involved with a very dangerous Philistine woman.

Samson fell in love ... The woman lived in the Valley of Sorek. Her name was Delilah.

The rulers of the Philistines went to her. They said, "See if you can get him to tell you the secret of why he's so strong. Find out how we can overpower him. Then we can tie him up. We can bring him under our control. Each of us will give you 28 pounds of silver."

So Delilah spoke to Samson. She said, "Tell me the secret of why you are so strong. Tell me how you can be tied up and controlled."

Samson answered her, "Let someone tie me up with seven new leather straps. They must be straps that aren't completely dry. Then I'll become as weak as any other man."

So the Philistine rulers brought seven new leather straps to her. They weren't completely dry. Delilah tied Samson up with them.

Men were hiding in the room. She called out to him. She said, "Samson! The Philistines are attacking you!" But he snapped the leather straps easily. They were like pieces of string that had come too close to a flame. So the secret of why he was so strong wasn't discovered.

Delilah spoke to Samson again. "You have made me look foolish," she said. "You told me a lie. Come on. Tell me how you can be tied up."

Samson said, "Let someone tie me tightly with new ropes. They must be ropes that have never been used. Then I'll become as weak as any other man."

So Delilah got some new ropes. She tied him up with them. Men were hiding in the room. She called out to him. She said, "Samson! The Philistines are attacking you!" But he snapped the ropes off his arms. They fell off just as if they were threads.

Delilah spoke to Samson again. "Until now, you have been making me look foolish," she said. "You have been telling me lies. This time really tell me how you can be tied up."

He replied, "Weave the seven braids of my hair into the cloth on a loom. Then pin my hair to the loom. If you do, I'll become as weak as any other man."

So while Samson was sleeping, Delilah took hold of the seven braids of his hair. She wove them into the cloth on a loom. Then she pinned his hair to the loom.

Again she called out to him. She said, "Samson! The Philistines are attacking you!" He woke up from his sleep. He pulled up the pin and the loom, together with the cloth.

Then she said to him, "How can you say, 'I love you'? You won't even share your secret with me. This is the third time you have made me look foolish. And you still haven't told me the secret of why you are so strong."

She continued to pester him day after day. She nagged him until he was sick and tired of it.

So he told her everything. "I've never used a razor on my head," he said. "I've never cut my hair. That's because I've been a Nazirite since the day I was born. A Nazirite is set apart to God. If you shave my head, I won't be strong anymore. I'll become as weak as any other man."

Delilah realized he had told her everything. So she sent a message to the Philistine rulers. She said, "Come back one more time. He has told me everything." So the rulers returned. They brought the silver with them.

Delilah got Samson to go to sleep on her lap. Then she called for a man to shave off the seven braids of his hair. That's how she began to bring him under her control. And he wasn't strong anymore.

She called out, "Samson! The Philistines are attacking you!"

He woke up from his sleep. He thought, "I'll go out just as I did before. I'll shake myself free." But he didn't know that the LORD had left him.

Then the Philistines grabbed hold of him. They poked his eyes out. They took him down to Gaza. They put bronze chains around him. Then they made him grind grain in the prison. His head had been shaved. But the hair on it began to grow again.

The rulers of the Philistines gathered together. They were going to offer a great sacrifice to their god Dagon. They were going to celebrate. They said, "Our god has handed our enemy Samson over to us."

When the people saw Samson, they praised their god. They said,

"Our god has handed our enemy over to us …

"Bring Samson out. Let him put on a show for us." So they called Samson out of the prison. He put on a show for them.

They had him stand near the temple pillars. Then he spoke to the servant who was holding his hand. He said, "Put me

where I can feel the pillars. I'm talking about the ones that hold the temple up. I want to lean against them."

Then he prayed to the LORD. He said, "LORD and King, show me that you still have concern for me. God, please make me strong just one more time ... "

Then Samson reached toward the two pillars that were in the middle of the temple. They held the temple up. He put his right hand on one of them. He put his left hand on the other. He leaned hard against them ...

Then he pushed with all his might. The temple came down on the rulers. It fell on all of the people who were in it. So Samson killed many more Philistines when he died than he did while he lived.

Samson was considered a hero to God's people because of what he did. Even though he didn't live up to his great gifts all the time, God still used him to fulfill God's plan.

Discussion Questions

1. If you could have a super power (like super-human strength or being able to walk up the sides of 100-story buildings), what would you choose? Why would you choose that power?
2. How do you feel when people tell one of your secrets to others?
3. How can you be a good brother, sister, or neighbor?

9

The Faith of a Foreign Woman

After Samson, the Israelites again started to sin and worship idols. A famine was going on in Judah, and no food would grow, so the people were always very hungry. A woman named Naomi and her family moved to the country of Moab where there was food. But when they got to Moab, Naomi's husband died. Her sons got married in Moab to women named Orpah and Ruth. But then Naomi's sons died, and she couldn't live in Moab anymore. Back then, widows had to be cared for by male relatives. All of Naomi's relatives lived back in Israel.

While Naomi was in Moab, she heard that the LORD had helped his people. He had begun to provide food for them again. So Naomi and her daughters-in-law prepared to go from Moab back to her home. She left the place where she had been living. Her two daughters-in-law went with her. They started out on the road that would take them back to the land of Judah.

Naomi spoke to her two daughters-in-law. "Both of you go back," she said. "Each of you go to your own mother's home. You were kind to your husbands, who have died. You have also been kind to me. So may the LORD be just as kind to you. May he help each of you find a secure place in the home of another husband. May he give you peace and rest."

Then she kissed them good-by. They broke down and sobbed loudly. They said to her, "We'll go back to your people with you."

But Naomi said, "Go home, my daughters. Why would you want to come with me? Am I going to have any more sons who could become your husbands?

"Go home, my daughters. I'm too old to have another husband. Suppose I thought there was still some hope for me. Suppose I got married to a man tonight. And later I had sons by him. Would you wait until they grew up? Would you stay single until you could get married to them? No, my daughters. My life is more bitter than yours. The LORD's powerful hand has been against me!"

When they heard that, they broke down and sobbed again. Then Orpah kissed her mother-in-law good-by. But Ruth held on to her.

"Look," said Naomi. "Your sister-in-law is going back to her people and her gods. Go back with her."

But Ruth replied, "Don't try to make me leave you and go back. Where you go I'll go. Where you stay I'll stay. Your people will be my people. Your God will be my God. Where you die I'll die. And there my body will be buried. I won't let anything except death separate you from me. If I do, may the LORD punish me greatly."

Naomi realized that Ruth had made up her mind to go with her. So she stopped trying to make her go back.

The two women continued on their way. At last they arrived in Bethlehem.

Ruth, who was from Moab, spoke to Naomi. She said, "Let me go out to the fields. I'll pick up the grain that has been left. I'll do it behind anyone who is pleased with me."

Naomi said to her, "My daughter, go ahead."

So Ruth went out and began to pick up grain. She worked in the fields behind those who were cutting and gathering the grain. As it turned out, she was working in a field that belonged to Boaz …

Just then Boaz arrived from Bethlehem. He greeted those who were cutting and gathering the grain. He said, "May the LORD be with you!"

"And may the LORD bless you!" they replied.

Boaz spoke to the man who was in charge of his workers. He asked, "Who is that young woman?"

The man replied, "She's from Moab. She came back from there with Naomi. She said, 'Please let me walk behind the workers. Let me pick up the grain that is left.' Then she went into the field. She has kept on working there from morning until now. She took only one short rest in the shade."

So Boaz said to Ruth, "Dear woman, listen to me. Don't pick up grain in any other field. Don't go anywhere else. Stay here with my female servants. Keep your eye on the field where the men are cutting grain. Walk behind the women who are gathering it. Pick up the grain that is left. I've told the men not to touch you. When you are thirsty, go and get a drink. Take water from the jars the men have filled."

When Ruth heard that, she bowed down with her face to the ground. She asked, "Why are you being so kind to me? In fact, why are you even noticing me? I'm from another country."

Boaz replied, "I've been told all about you. I've heard about everything you have done for your mother-in-law since your

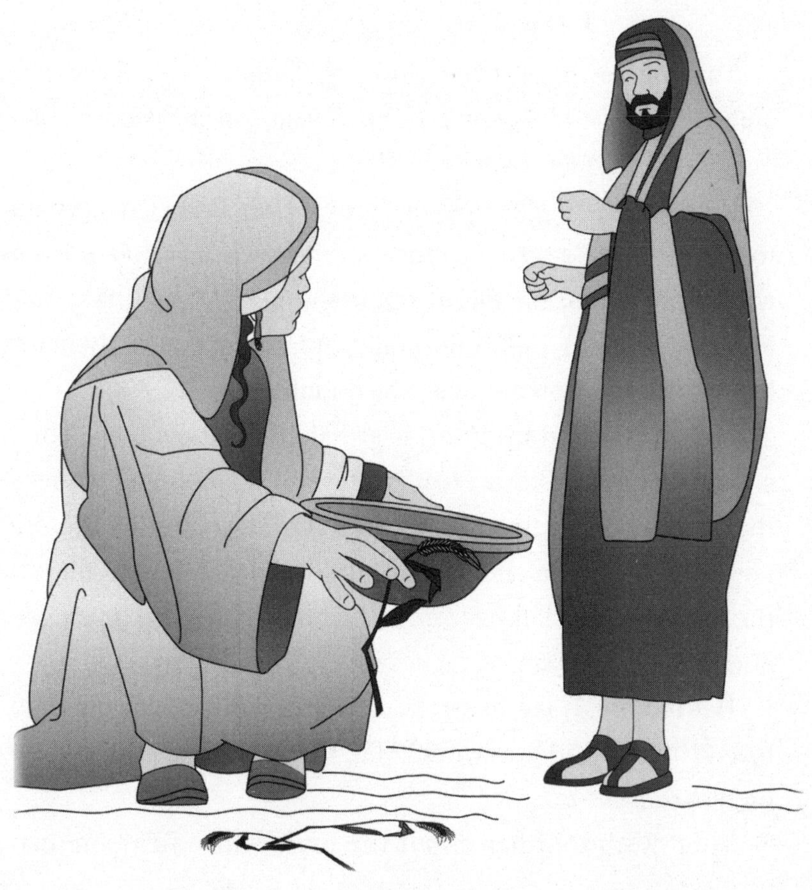

husband died. I know that you left your father and mother. I know that you left your country. You came to live with people you didn't know before.

"May the LORD reward you for what you have done. May the God of Israel bless you richly. You have come to him to find safety under his care."

"Sir, I hope you will continue to be kind to me," Ruth said. "You have comforted me. You have spoken kindly to me. And I'm not even as important as one of your female servants!"

When it was time to eat, Boaz spoke to Ruth again. "Come over here," he said. "Have some bread. Dip it in the wine vinegar."

She sat down with the workers. Then Boaz offered her some grain that had been cooked. She ate all she wanted. She even had some left over.

Ruth got up to pick up more grain. Then Boaz gave orders to his men. He said, "Suppose she takes some stalks from what the women have tied up. If she does, don't make her look bad. Instead, pull some stalks out for her. Leave them for her to pick up. Don't tell her she shouldn't do it."

So Ruth picked up grain in the field until evening. Then she separated the barley from the straw. It amounted to more than half a bushel. She carried it back to town. Her mother-in-law saw how much she had gathered. Ruth also brought out the food that was left over from the lunch Boaz had given her. She gave it to Naomi.

Her mother-in-law asked her, "Where did you pick up grain today? Where did you work? May the man who noticed you be blessed!"

Then Ruth told her about the man whose field she had

worked in. "The name of the man I worked with today is Boaz," she said.

"May the LORD bless him!" Naomi said to her daughter-in-law. "The LORD is still being kind to those who are living and those who are dead."

She continued, "That man is a close relative of ours. He's one of our family protectors."

Then Ruth, who was from Moab, said, "He told me more. He even said, 'Stay with my workers until they have finished bringing in all of my grain.' "

Naomi replied to her daughter-in-law Ruth. She said, "That will be good for you, my daughter. Go with his female servants. You might be harmed if you go to someone else's field."

So Ruth stayed close to the female servants of Boaz as she picked up grain. She worked until the time when all of the barley and wheat had been harvested. And she lived with her mother-in-law.

Boaz continued to be kind to Ruth. Because he was a close relative, he took care of Ruth and Naomi. He made arrangements to marry Ruth.

So Boaz got married to Ruth. She became his wife ... The LORD blessed her so that she became pregnant. And she had a son.

The women said to Naomi, "We praise the LORD. Today he has provided a family protector for you. May this child become famous all over Israel! He will make your life new again. He'll take care of you when you are old. He's the son of your very own daughter-in-law. She loves you. She is better to you than seven sons."

Then Naomi put the child on her lap and took care of him. The women who were living there said, "Naomi has a son." They named him Obed. He was the father of Jesse. Jesse was the father of David.

Discussion Questions

1. Do you share things with your friends? What types of things do you share? When was the last time you shared?

2. Do you have a friend you can rely on when you have problems? What makes that person trustworthy? Can that friend rely on you too?

3. Have you ever given up something to help a friend? What happened?

10

Messages from God

Hannah's husband loved her very much. But she was always sad because she couldn't have a baby. Hannah went to God's house to pray and ask him to give her a baby.

Hannah was very bitter. She sobbed and sobbed. She prayed to the LORD. She made a promise to him. She said, "LORD, you rule over all. Please see how I'm suffering! Show concern for me! Don't forget about me! Please give me a son! If you do, I'll give him back to you. Then he will serve you all the days of his life. He'll never use a razor on his head. He'll never cut his hair."

As Hannah kept on praying to the LORD, Eli watched her lips. She was praying in her heart. Her lips were moving. But she wasn't making a sound.

The person who took care of God's house was named Eli. When he saw Hannah praying, he didn't know what she was doing and thought she was drunk, so he was upset with her. Hannah explained.

"I'm a woman who is deeply troubled ... I was telling the LORD all of my troubles. Don't think of me as an evil woman. I've been praying here because I'm very sad. My pain is so great."

Eli answered, "Go in peace. May the God of Israel give you what you have asked him for."

She said, "May you be pleased with me." Then she left and had something to eat. Her face wasn't sad anymore.

After some time, Hannah became pregnant. She had a baby boy. She said, "I asked the LORD for him." So she named him Samuel.

Hannah was very, very happy when Samuel was born. She loved him very much and took care of him at her house until he wasn't a baby anymore. But she knew Samuel couldn't live with her forever—after all, she'd promised God that Samuel would serve him all his life.

Hannah brought the boy to Eli. Hannah said to Eli, "Sir, I'm the woman who stood here beside you praying to the LORD. And that's just as sure as you are alive. I prayed for this child. The LORD has given me what I asked him for. So now I'm giving him to the LORD. As long as he lives he'll be given to the LORD." And all of them worshiped the LORD there.

Then Hannah prayed. She said,

"The LORD has filled my heart with joy.
He has made me strong.

I can laugh at my enemies.
    I'm so glad he saved me.

There isn't anyone holy like the LORD.
    There isn't anyone except him.
    There isn't any Rock like our God."

The LORD was gracious to Hannah. She became pregnant. Over a period of years she had three more sons and two daughters. During that whole time the boy Samuel grew up serving the LORD.

The boy Samuel served the LORD under the direction of Eli. In those days the LORD didn't give many messages to his people. He didn't give them many visions.

One night Eli was lying down in his usual place. His eyes were becoming so weak he couldn't see very well. Samuel was lying down in the LORD's house. That's where the ark of God was kept. The lamp of God was still burning. The LORD called out to Samuel.

Samuel answered, "Here I am." He ran over to Eli. He said, "Here I am. You called out to me."

But Eli said, "I didn't call you. Go back and lie down." So he went and lay down.

Again the LORD called out, "Samuel!" Samuel got up and went to Eli. He said, "Here I am. You called out to me."

"My son," Eli said, "I didn't call you. Go back and lie down."

Samuel didn't know the LORD yet. That's because the LORD still hadn't given him a message.

The LORD called out to Samuel for the third time. Samuel got up and went to Eli. He said, "Here I am. You called out to me."

Then Eli realized that the LORD was calling the boy. So Eli told Samuel, "Go and lie down. If someone calls out to you again, say, 'Speak, LORD. I'm listening.'" So Samuel went and lay down in his place.

The LORD came and stood there. He called out, just as he had done the other times. He said, "Samuel! Samuel!"

Then Samuel replied, "Speak. I'm listening."

God knew that the Israelites needed someone to lead them, and he chose Samuel for the task. As Samuel grew up, he and God talked all the time. Samuel would tell the Israelites what God said, and the people would listen. Samuel was a very good man, and he did what God wanted.

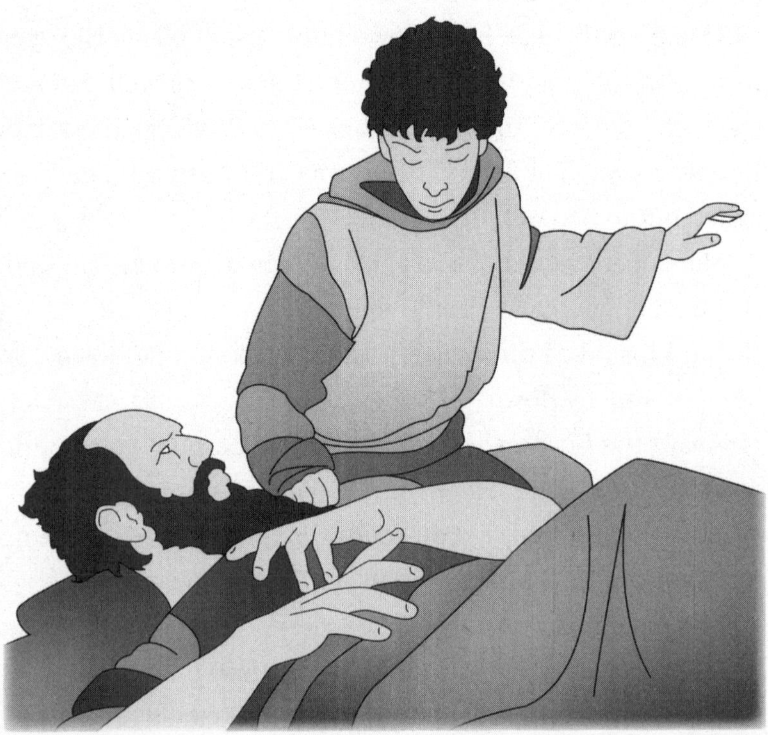

When Samuel became old, he appointed his sons to serve as judges for Israel.

But his sons didn't live as he did. They were only interested in making money. They accepted money from people who wanted special favors. They made things that were wrong appear to be right.

So all of the elders of Israel gathered together. They came to Samuel at Ramah. They said to him, "You are old. Your sons don't live as you do. So appoint a king to lead us. We want a king just like the kings all of the other nations have."

Samuel wasn't pleased when they said, "Give us a king to lead us." So he prayed to the LORD.

The LORD told him, "Listen to everything the people are saying to you. You are not the one they have turned their backs on. I am the one they do not want as their king. They are doing just as they have always done. They have deserted me and served other gods. They have done that from the time I brought them up out of Egypt until this very day. Now they are deserting you too.

"Let them have what they want. But give them a strong warning. Let them know what the king who rules over them will do."

Samuel told the people who were asking him for a king everything the LORD had said. Samuel told them, "Here's what the king who rules over you will do. He will take your sons. He'll make them serve with his chariots and horses. They will run in front of his chariots. He'll choose some of your sons to be commanders of thousands of men. Some will be commanders of fifties. Others will have to plow his fields and gather his crops. Still others will have to make weapons of war and parts for his chariots.

"He'll also take your daughters. Some will have to make perfume. Others will be forced to cook and bake.

"He will take away your best fields and vineyards and olive groves. He'll give them to his attendants. He will take a tenth of your grain and a tenth of your grapes. He'll give it to his officials and attendants. He will also take your male and female servants. He'll take your best cattle and donkeys. He'll use all of them any way he wants to.

"He will take a tenth of your sheep and goats. You yourselves will become his slaves.

"When that time comes, you will cry out for help because of the king you have chosen. But the LORD won't answer you at that time."

In spite of what Samuel said, the people refused to listen to him. "No!" they said. "We want a king to rule over us. Then we'll be like all of the other nations. We'll have a king to lead us. He'll go out at the head of our armies and fight our battles."

Samuel heard everything the people said. He told the LORD about it. The LORD answered, "Listen to them. Give them a king."

In Israel, God was supposed to be the king. But the Israelites wanted a human king, like the other countries around them. God knew that a king would make life hard for his people, but he told Samuel that he would let Israel have a human king. God chose a man named Saul to be the first king. Saul came to Samuel to ask him to help him locate some lost donkeys. While Saul was with him, Samuel anointed him king.

The LORD had spoken to Samuel the day before Saul came. He had said, "About this time tomorrow I will send you a man. He is from the land of Benjamin. Anoint him to be the leader of my people Israel. He will save them from the powerful hand of the Philistines. I have seen how much my people are suffering. Their cry for help has reached me."

When Samuel saw a man coming toward him, the LORD spoke to Samuel again. He said, "He is the man I told you about. His name is Saul. He will govern my people."

Saul approached Samuel at the gate of the town. He asked Samuel, "Can you please show me the house where the seer is staying?"

"I'm the seer," Samuel replied. "Go on up to the high place ahead of me. I want you and your servant to eat with me today. Tomorrow morning I'll tell you what's on your mind. Then I'll let you go. Don't worry about the donkeys you lost three days ago. They've already been found. But who are all of the people of Israel longing for? You and your father's whole family!"

Saul answered, "But I'm from the tribe of Benjamin. It's the smallest tribe in Israel. And my family group is the least important in the whole tribe of Benjamin. So why are you saying that to me?"

Then Samuel took a bottle of olive oil. He poured it on Saul's head and kissed him. He said, "The LORD has anointed you to be the leader of his people. When you leave me today, you will meet two men ... They'll say to you, 'The donkeys you have been looking for have been found. Now your father has stopped thinking about them. Instead, he's worried about you. He's asking, "What can I do to find my son?"'

"After that, you will go to Gibeah of God. Some Philistine soldiers are stationed there. As you approach the town, you will meet a group of prophets. They'll be coming down from the high place where they worship. People will be playing lyres, tambourines, flutes and harps at the head of the group. The prophets will be prophesying. The Spirit of the LORD will come on you with power. Then you will prophesy along with them. You will become a different person.

"All of those things will happen. Then do what you want to do. God is with you."

As Saul turned to leave Samuel, God changed Saul's heart. All of those things happened that day.

At first, Saul was a very good king. The Spirit God sent to Saul made him brave, smart, and a good leader. But before long Saul started to do things God told him not to do. God decided he didn't want Saul to be king anymore. He took away the Spirit that made Saul a good king, and God told Samuel to look for a new king—a king who loved God more than anything and would always try to do what God wanted.

Discussion Questions

1. Have you ever wanted something so badly that you became upset when you didn't get it? What did you want but not get? How did you resolve your problem?

2. What can you do to serve God? Describe three ways.

11

From Shepherd to King

God knew who he wanted to be the new king of Israel, so he sent Samuel to Bethlehem to secretly anoint the new king. When Samuel got there, he couldn't believe who God had picked—not a tall, strong man, but a shepherd named David!

Even though David was the king God wanted, nobody but Samuel, David and David's family knew. God wanted to wait until the right time to make David the official king of Israel. Saul was still king—and he and the Israelites were fighting the Philistines.

The Philistines gathered their army together for war ... Saul and the army of Israel gathered together. They camped in the Valley of Elah. They lined up their men to fight against the Philistines. The Philistine army was camped on one hill. Israel's army was on another. The valley was between them.

A mighty hero named Goliath came out of the Philistine camp. He was from Gath. He was more than nine feet tall. He had a bronze helmet on his head. He wore a coat of bronze armor. It weighed 125 pounds. On his legs he wore bronze guards. He carried a bronze javelin on his back. His spear was as big as a weaver's rod. Its iron point weighed 15 pounds.

Goliath stood and shouted to the soldiers of Israel. He said, "Why do you come out and line up for battle? I'm a Philistine. You are servants of Saul. Choose one of your men. Have him come down and face me."

For forty days Goliath dared anyone from the Israelite army to fight him. And every time Saul and his army looked at Goliath and his big spear, they started shaking. David's brothers were in Saul's army, and their father, Jesse, wanted to send them some supplies.

Early in the morning David left his father's flock in the care of a shepherd. David loaded up the food and started out, just as Jesse had directed.

David reached the camp as the army was going out to its battle positions. The soldiers were shouting the war cry. Israel and the Philistines were lining up their armies for battle. The armies were facing each other.

David left what he had brought with the man who took care of the supplies. He ran to the battle lines and greeted his brothers. As David was talking with them, Goliath stepped forward from his line. Goliath was a mighty Philistine hero from Gath. He again dared someone to fight him, and David heard it.

When Israel's army saw Goliath, all of them ran away from him. That's because they were filled with fear.

David asked the men, "Who does that bully think he is? We have God on our side!" David had faith that God would watch over him.

David's oldest brother Eliab heard him speaking with the men. So he burned with anger at him. He asked him, "Why have you come down here? Who did you leave those few sheep in the desert with? I know how proud you are. I know how evil your heart is. The only reason you came down here was to watch the battle."

"What have I done now?" said David. "Can't I even speak?"

Then he turned away to speak to some other men. He asked them the same question he had asked before. And they gave him the same answer.

Someone heard what David said and reported it to Saul. So Saul sent for him.

David said to Saul, "Don't let anyone lose hope because of that Philistine. I'll go out and fight him."

Saul replied, "You aren't able to go out there and fight that Philistine. You are too young. He's been a fighting man ever since he was a boy."

But David said to Saul, "I've been taking care of my father's sheep. Sometimes a lion or a bear would come and carry off a sheep from the flock. Then I would go after it and hit it. I would save the sheep it was carrying in its mouth.

"The Lord saved me from the paw of the lion. He saved me from the paw of the bear. And he'll save me from the powerful hand of this Philistine too."

Saul said to David, "Go. And may the LORD be with you."

Then David picked up his wooden staff. He went down to a stream and chose five smooth stones. He put them in the pocket of his shepherd's bag. Then he took his sling in his hand and approached Goliath.

At that same time, the Philistine kept coming closer to David. The man who was carrying Goliath's shield walked along in front of him.

Goliath looked David over. He saw how young he was. He also saw how tanned and handsome he was. And he hated him. He said to David, "Why are you coming at me with sticks? Do you think I'm only a dog?" The Philistine called down curses on David in the name of his god. "Come over here," he said. "I'll feed your body to the birds of the air! I'll feed it to the wild animals!"

David said to Goliath, "You are coming to fight against me with a sword, a spear and a javelin. But I'm coming against you in the name of the LORD who rules over all. He is the God of the armies of Israel. He's the one you have dared to fight against.

"This very day the LORD will hand you over to me. I'll strike you down ... Then the whole world will know there is a God in Israel.

"The LORD doesn't save by using a sword or a spear. And everyone who is here will know it. The battle belongs to the LORD. He will hand all of you over to us."

As the Philistine moved closer to attack him, David ran quickly to the battle line to meet him. He reached into his bag. He took out a stone. He put it in his sling. He slung it at

Goliath. The stone hit him on the forehead and sank into it. He fell to the ground on his face.

David defeated Goliath with God's help, and the Philistines ran away. David became a hero. Soon songs were written that said how much better David was than Saul. Saul was furious that David was getting so much attention, and he was afraid the people would want David to be their king instead. Saul decided to kill David. After dodging a few spears and finding out about Saul's plans, David went into hiding and prayed to God for protection.

Here's a psalm (or song) that David wrote while he was hiding from Saul:

God, save me from my enemies.
    Keep me safe from those who rise up against me.
Save me from those who do evil.
    Save me from murderers.

See how they hide and wait for me!
    LORD, angry people plan to harm me,
    even though I haven't hurt them in any way or sinned
        against them.
I haven't done anything wrong to them. But they are
        ready to attack me.
    Rise up and help me! Look at what I'm up against!
LORD God who rules over all, rise up. God of Israel,
        punish all of the nations.

You give me strength. I look to you.
    God, you are like a fort to me. You are my loving God.
But I will sing about your strength.
    In the morning I will sing about your love.
You are like a fort to me.
    You keep me safe in times of trouble.

You give me strength. I sing praise to you.
    God, you are like a fort to me. You are my loving God.

David really loved and trusted God for everything, and he knew God would take care of him as he hid from Saul. No matter where David went or what trouble he faced, God was watching out for David. When Saul died, God made David king of Israel, and God promised that one of David's descendents would always be king. Because David was such a good king, God blessed David and his entire kingdom.

Discussion Questions

1. Do you get along with your brother or sister most of the time? (If you don't have any siblings, do you get along with your friends?) Can you name two ways to get along with them better?
2. Have you ever had to face a bully or a big problem? What did you do? Did you ask anyone for help?
3. David praised God by writing psalms. How can you praise God?

12

A King Makes Bad Choices

David tried to do what God wanted him to do, but he made a terrible mistake when he saw a woman named Bathsheba. She was married, but David wanted her to be his wife—so he had her husband go into battle where he was killed. Then David married Bathsheba.

God told David that what he had done was very wrong and that David would be punished for his sin. David wrote this song, called a psalm, to help him deal with God's punishment and to ask for forgiveness for what he did.

God, show me your favor
  in keeping with your faithful love.
Because your love is so tender and kind,
  wipe out my lawless acts.

Wash away all of the evil things I've done.
  Make me pure from my sin.

I know the lawless acts I've committed.
  I can't forget my sin.
You are the one I've really sinned against.
  I've done what is evil in your sight.
So you are right when you sentence me.
  You are fair when you judge me.
I know I've been a sinner ever since I was born.
  I've been a sinner ever since my mother became pregnant with me.
I know that you want truth to be in my heart.
  You teach me wisdom deep down inside me.

Make me pure by sprinkling me with hyssop plant. Then I will be clean.
  Wash me. Then I will be whiter than snow.
Let me hear you say, "Your sins are forgiven."
  That will bring me joy and gladness.
  Let the body you have broken be glad.
Take away all of my sins.
  Wipe away all of the evil things I've done.

God, create a pure heart in me.
  Give me a new spirit that is faithful to you.
Don't send me away from you.
  Don't take your Holy Spirit away from me.
Give me back the joy that comes from being saved by you.
  Give me a spirit that obeys you. That will keep me going.

Sinful people have all kinds of trouble.
But the LORD's faithful love is all around those who trust in him.

Be glad because of what the LORD has done for you.
Be joyful, you who do what is right!
Sing, all of you whose hearts are honest!

God forgave David, and David again obeyed God. Bathsheba had a baby who they named Solomon. This was a happy time in David's palace, but the happy times didn't last very long.

One of David's sons, named Absalom, decided he should be king instead of David. He went to war against his father to take over the kingdom. In one of the battles, Absalom died, and David was very sad.

Throughout all his hardships, David still loved and worshiped God and wanted to do something special for God—to build a beautiful temple for him.

King David spoke to the whole community. He said, "God has chosen my son Solomon. But Solomon is young. He's never done anything like this before. The task is huge. This grand and wonderful temple won't be built for human beings. It will be built for the LORD God.

"With all of my riches I've done everything I could for the temple of my God. I've provided gold for the gold work and silver for the silver work. I've provided bronze for the bronze work and iron for the iron work. I've given wood for the things that will be made out of wood. I've given onyx and turquoise for the settings. I've given stones of different colors and all kinds of fine stone and marble. I've provided everything in huge amounts.

"With all my heart I want the temple of my God to be built. So I'm giving my personal treasures of gold and silver for it. I'm adding them to everything else I've provided for the holy temple ... How many of you are willing to set yourselves apart to the LORD today?"

Many people were willing to give. They included the leaders of families and the officers of the tribes of Israel. They included the commanders of thousands of men and commanders of hundreds. They also included the officials who were in charge of the king's work.

The people were happy when they saw what their leaders had been willing to give. The leaders had given freely. With their whole heart they had given everything to the LORD. King David was filled with joy.

David praised the LORD in front of the whole community. He said,

"LORD, we give you praise.
    You are the God of our father Israel.
    We give you praise for ever and ever.
LORD, you are great and powerful.
    Glory, majesty and beauty belong to you.
    Everything in heaven and on earth belongs to you.
LORD, the kingdom belongs to you.
    You are honored as the One who rules over all.
Wealth and honor come from you.
    You are the ruler of all things.
In your hands are strength and power.
    You can give honor and strength to everyone.
Our God, we give you thanks.
    We praise your glorious name.

"My God, I know that you put our hearts to the test. And you are pleased when we are honest. I've given all of these things just because I wanted to. When I did it, I was completely honest with you. And I've been happy to see that your people who are here have also been willing to give to you.

"LORD, you are the God of our fathers Abraham, Isaac and Israel. Keep this longing in the hearts of your people forever. Keep their hearts true to you. Help my son Solomon serve you with all his heart. Then he will keep your commands and rules. He will do what you require. He'll do everything to build the grand and wonderful temple I've provided for."

Then David spoke to the whole community. He said, "Praise the LORD your God." So all of them praised the LORD. He's the God of their people who lived long ago. The whole community bowed low. They fell down flat with their faces toward the ground. They did it in front of the LORD and the king.

David was an amazing man. He was a warrior who won many battles, he was one of the best kings Israel ever had, he designed the temple, and he was an excellent musician. There are 73 of David's psalms in the Bible. The most famous one is Psalm 23 which reads like this:

The LORD is my shepherd. He gives me everything I need.
He lets me lie down in fields of green grass.
He leads me beside quiet waters.
He gives me new strength.
He guides me in the right paths
for the honor of his name.
Even though I walk
through the darkest valley,
I will not be afraid.
You are with me.
Your shepherd's rod and staff
comfort me.

You prepare a feast for me
right in front of my enemies.
You pour oil on my head.
My cup runs over.

I am sure that your goodness and love will follow me
all the days of my life.
And I will live in the house of the Lord
forever.

Discussion Questions

1. David played a harp. Do you play a musical instrument or sing? If not, what are some God-given talents that you have? What do you think God would like you to do with these talents?

2. Have you ever asked God to forgive you? Do you think he forgave you? Why?

13

The King Who Had It All

David was king for forty years, and he did an excellent job leading Israel. He was getting very old, and it was time to hand over the kingdom to his son, Solomon. Before David died, he gave Solomon the plans for the temple and instructions to always obey God.

Solomon was a very different king than David. The people lived in peace with all the nations around them. There were no more wars. Solomon made his kingdom great by using the wisdom God had given him.

Solomon and Pharaoh, the king of Egypt, agreed to help each other. So Solomon got married to Pharaoh's daughter. He brought her to the City of David. She stayed there until he finished building his palace, the LORD's temple, and the wall that was around Jerusalem.

But the people continued to offer sacrifices at the high places where they worshiped. That's because a temple hadn't been built yet where the LORD would put his Name.

Solomon showed his love for the LORD. He did it by obeying the laws his father David had taught him. But Solomon offered sacrifices at the high places. He also burned incense there.

King Solomon went to the city of Gibeon to offer sacrifices. That's where the most important high place was. He offered 1,000 burnt offerings on the altar that was there.

The LORD appeared to Solomon at Gibeon. He spoke to him in a dream during the night. God said, "Ask for anything you want me to give you."

Solomon answered, "You have been very kind to my father David, your servant. That's because he was faithful to you. He did what was right. His heart was honest. And you have continued to be very kind to him. You have given him a son to sit on his throne this very day.

"LORD my God, you have now made me king. You have put me in the place of my father David. But I'm only a little child. I don't know how to carry out my duties. I'm here among the people you have chosen. They are a great nation. They are more than anyone can count. So give me a heart that understands. Then I can rule over your people. I can tell the difference between what is right and what is wrong. Who can possibly rule over this great nation of yours?"

The Lord was pleased that Solomon had asked for that. So God said to him, "You have not asked to live for a long time. You have not asked to be wealthy. You have not even asked to have your enemies killed. Instead, you have asked for understanding. You want to do what is right and fair when you judge people. Because that is what you have asked for, I will give it to you. I will give you a wise and understanding heart. So here is what will be true of you. There has never been anyone like you. And there never will be.

"And that is not all. I will give you what you have not asked for. I will give you riches and honor. As long as you live, no other king will be as great as you are. Live the way I want you to. Obey my laws and commands, just as your father David did. Then I will let you live for a long time."

Solomon woke up. He realized he had been dreaming.

He returned to Jerusalem. He stood in front of the ark of the LORD's covenant. He sacrificed burnt offerings and friendship offerings. Then he gave a big dinner for all of his officials.

God made Solomon very wise. His understanding couldn't even be measured. It was like the sand on the seashore. People can't measure that either.

Solomon's wisdom was greater than the wisdom of all of the people of the east. It was greater than all of the wisdom of Egypt.

Solomon was constantly thinking of wise things that people needed to know. Many of his wise sayings are included in the book of the Bible called Proverbs. Here is some of what he wrote:

Proverbs teach you wisdom and train you.
    They help you understand wise sayings.
They provide you with training and help you live wisely.
    They lead to what is right and honest and fair.

They give understanding to childish people.
They give knowledge and good sense to those who are young.

If you really want to gain knowledge, you must begin by having respect for the LORD.
But foolish people hate wisdom and training.

My son, do not forget my teaching.
Keep my commands in your heart.
They will help you live for many years.
They will bring you success.

Don't let love and truth ever leave you.
Tie them around your neck.
Write them on the tablet of your heart.
Then you will find favor and a good name
in the eyes of God and people.

Trust in the LORD with all your heart.
Do not depend on your own understanding.
In all your ways remember him.
Then he will make your paths smooth and straight.

Don't be wise in your own eyes.
Have respect for the LORD and avoid evil.
That will bring health to your body.
It will make your bones strong.

Honor the LORD with your wealth.

The LORD trains those he loves.
He is like a father who trains the son he is pleased with.

There is gold. There are plenty of rubies.
But lips that speak knowledge are a priceless jewel.

Food gained by cheating tastes sweet to a man.
But he will end up with a mouth full of sand.

Anyone who is careful about what he says
keeps himself out of trouble.
No wisdom, wise saying or plan
can succeed against the LORD.

You can prepare a horse for the day of battle.
But the power to win comes from the LORD.

King Solomon was the king entrusted to build God's temple. For seven years, thousands of men cut logs, melted gold, and sculpted furniture to complete the temple. It was a huge, impressive place where God could be worshiped.

After the temple was finished, Solomon asked all the leaders in Israel to come and bring the ark of the covenant. Once the ark was in place, God entered the temple, making it the official place to worship him.

Then Solomon stood in front of the LORD's altar. He stood in front of the whole community of Israel. He spread out his hands toward heaven. He said,

"LORD, you are the God of Israel. There is no God like you in heaven above or on earth below. You keep the covenant you made with us. You show us your love. You do that when we follow you with all our hearts. You have kept your promise to my father David. He was your servant. With your mouth you made a promise. With your powerful hand you have made it come true. And today we can see it.

"But will you really live on earth? After all, the heavens can't hold you. In fact, even the highest heavens can't hold you. So this temple I've built certainly can't hold you!

"But please pay attention to my prayer. LORD my God, show me your favor as I make my appeal to you. Listen to my cry for help. Hear the prayer I'm praying to you today. Let your eyes look toward this temple night and day. You said, 'I will put my Name there.' So please listen to the prayer I'm praying toward this place.

"Hear me when I ask you to show us your favor. Listen to your people Israel when they pray toward this place. Listen to us from heaven. It's the place where you live. When you hear us, forgive us.

"My God, let your eyes see us. Let your ears pay attention to the prayers that are offered in this place.

"LORD God, rise up and come to your resting place.
Come in together with the ark.
It's the sign of your power.
LORD God, may your priests put on salvation as if it were their clothes.
May your faithful people be glad because you are so good.
LORD God, don't turn your back on your anointed king.
Remember the great love you promised to your servant David."

Solomon finished praying. Then fire came down from heaven. It burned up the burnt offering and the sacrifices. The glory of the LORD filled the temple. The priests couldn't enter the temple of the LORD. His glory filled it.

All of the people of Israel saw the fire coming down. They saw the glory of the LORD above the temple. So they got down on their knees in the courtyard with their faces toward the ground. They worshiped the LORD. They gave thanks to him. They said,

"He is good.
His faithful love continues forever."

Solomon built other things besides the temple; he built ships, palaces, huge stables and even an entire city. He made money by trading goods with people, and he shared his wisdom—he was the richest and most famous king in all the world. People from around the world came to Jerusalem to meet him.

The queen of Sheba heard about how famous Solomon was. She also heard about how he served and worshiped the LORD. So she came to test him with hard questions.

She arrived in Jerusalem with a very large group of attendants. Her camels were carrying spices, huge amounts of gold, and valuable jewels. She came to Solomon and asked him about everything she wanted to know.

Solomon answered all of her questions. There wasn't anything that was too hard for the king to explain to her.

So the queen of Sheba saw how very wise Solomon was. She saw the palace he had built.

She said to the king, "Back in my own country I heard a report about you. I heard about how much you had accomplished. I also heard about how wise you are. Everything I heard is true. But I didn't believe those things. So I came to see for myself. And now I believe it! You are twice as wise and wealthy as people say you are. The report I heard doesn't even begin to tell the whole story about you.

"How happy your men must be! How happy your officials must be! They always get to serve you and hear the wise things you say.

"May the LORD your God be praised. He must take great delight in you. He placed you on the throne of Israel. The LORD will love Israel for all time to come. That's why he has made you king. He knows that you will do what is fair and right."

The queen of Sheba came to Jerusalem because Solomon was very wise and loved God. But later Solomon started doing some very unwise things. He started worshiping idols instead of God.

The LORD became angry with Solomon. That's because his heart had turned away from the LORD. He is the God of Israel. He had appeared to Solomon twice. He had commanded Solomon not to follow other gods. But Solomon didn't obey him.

So the LORD said to Solomon, "You have chosen not to keep my covenant. You have decided not to obey my rules. I commanded you to do what I told you. But you did not do it. So you can be absolutely sure I will tear the kingdom away from you. I will give it to one of your officials.

"But I will not do that while you are still living. Because of your father David I will wait. I will tear the kingdom out of your son's hand. But I will not tear the whole kingdom away from him. I will give him one of the tribes because of my servant David. I will also do it because of Jerusalem. That is the city I have chosen."

Discussion Questions

1. If you could ask God for anything in the world, what would you ask him for? Why would you ask for this?

2. What are your favorite things to learn about? (Things like math, science, languages, art, music, sports?) What makes them interesting to you?

3. Solomon had a temple built for God. What could you build or make to show God how important he is to you?

14

A Kingdom Torn in Two

Because Solomon had not obeyed God and had stopped worshiping him, God planned to divide the kingdom in half. When Solomon died, his son Rehoboam became king of a small part of his father's kingdom. The large part was ruled by Jeroboam.

The country Rehoboam ruled was called Judah, and the kingdom Jeroboam ruled was called Israel. For the most part, the kings (and people) of Israel and Judah were very sinful.

The people of Judah did what was evil in the sight of the LORD. The sins they had committed stirred up his jealous anger. They did more to make him angry than their people who lived before them had done.

Judah also set up for themselves high places for worship. They set up sacred stones. They set up poles that were used to worship the goddess Asherah. They did it on every high hill and under every green tree.

When the people of Judah and Israel were sinful and didn't obey God, God would show them he was more powerful than their idols. God used evil kings from other countries, like Shishak of Egypt, to teach his people a lesson and make them come back to him.

[Shishak] carried away the treasures of the LORD's temple. He also carried the treasures of the royal palace away. He took everything. That included all of the gold shields Solomon had made.

So King Rehoboam made bronze shields to take their place. He gave them to the commanders of the guards who were on duty at the entrance to the royal palace. Every time the king went to the LORD's temple, the guards carried the shields. Later, they took them back to the room where they were kept.

In addition to a Pharaoh attacking Judah, Jeroboam and Rehoboam fought against each other. And when Rehoboam and Jeroboam died, their evil sons took over the kingdoms and continued to fight.

For the most part, Israel was very sinful. No matter who was king, the people kept sinning and worshiping idols, which made God angrier and angrier.

But there was still hope for Judah. Occasionally a king came to the throne who loved God and who tried to be a good king like David. Asa was one of these good kings.

Asa did what was right in the eyes of the LORD. That's what King David had done ...

He got rid of all of the statues of gods his people before him had made. He even removed his grandmother Maacah from her position as queen mother. That's because she had made a pole that was used to worship the goddess Asherah. The LORD hated it. So Asa cut it down. He burned it in the Kidron Valley.

Asa didn't remove the high places from Israel. But he committed his whole life completely to the LORD. He and his father had set apart silver, gold and other articles to the LORD. He brought them into the LORD's temple.

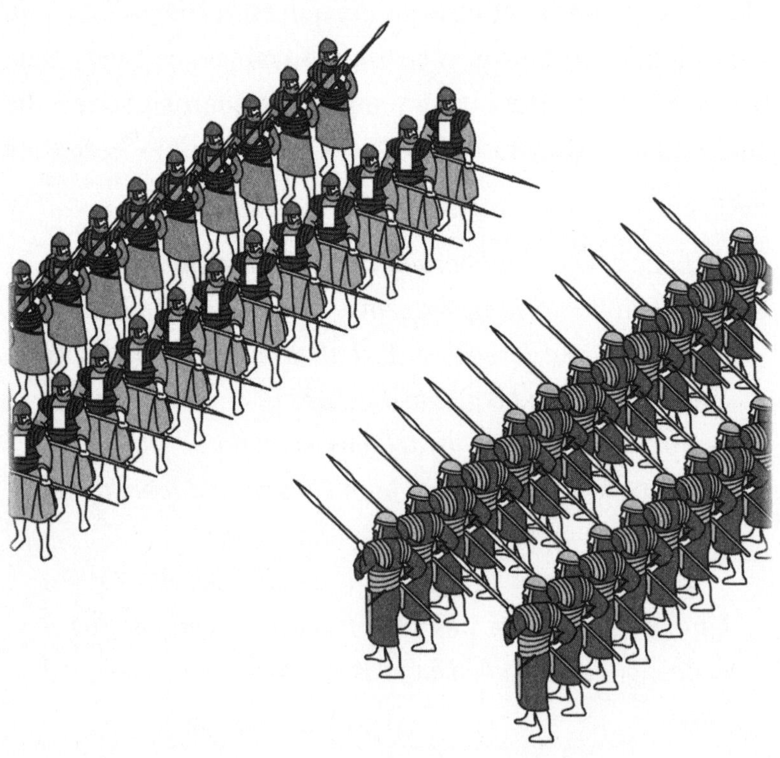

There was war between Asa and Baasha, the king of Israel. It lasted the whole time they were kings. Baasha was king of Israel. He marched out against Judah. He built up the walls of Ramah. He did it to keep people from leaving or entering the territory of Asa, the king of Judah.

Then King Asa gave an order to all of the men of Judah. Everyone was required to help. They carried away from Ramah the stones and wood Baasha had been using there. King Asa used them to build up Geba in the territory of Benjamin. He also used them to build up Mizpah.

All of the other events of Asa's rule are written down. Everything he accomplished is written down. Everything he did and the cities he built are written down. They are written in the official records of the kings of Judah. But when Asa became old, his feet began to give him trouble. He joined the members of his family who had already died. His body was buried in his family tomb. It was in the city of King David. Asa's son Jehoshaphat became the next king after him.

Asa and Jehoshaphat were good kings of Judah, but the kings in Israel were wicked. Several kings ruled in Israel after Baasha left the throne. Then the most evil, sinful, and idol-worshiping king came to the throne in Israel. His name was King Ahab.

Ahab, the son of Omri, did what was evil in the sight of the LORD. He did more evil things than any of the kings who had ruled before him. He thought it was only a small thing to commit the sins Jeroboam, the son of Nebat, had committed.

Ahab also got married to Jezebel ... Ahab began to serve

the god Baal and worship him. He set up an altar to honor Baal. He set it up in the temple of Baal that he built in Samaria. Ahab also made a pole that was used to worship the goddess Asherah.

He made the LORD very angry. He did more to make him angry than all of the kings of Israel had done before him.

Discussion Questions

1. Sometimes people don't follow God's rules. Which of God's rules are especially easy or hard for you to keep?
2. Describe some ways that people show God they love him. How do *you* show God that you love him?

15

God's Messengers

Elijah lived in Israel. He was as good and God-loving as King Ahab was evil and God-hating. Elijah was one of God's prophets, and God chose him to speak to Ahab.

[Elijah] said to Ahab, "I serve the LORD. He is the God of Israel. You can be sure that he lives. And you can be just as sure that there won't be any dew or rain on the whole land. There won't be any during the next few years. It won't come until I say so."

Then a message from the LORD came to Elijah. It said, "Leave this place. Go east and hide in the Kerith Valley. It is east of the Jordan River. You will drink water from the brook. I have ordered some ravens to feed you there."

So Elijah did what the LORD had told him to do. He went to the Kerith Valley. It was east of the Jordan River. He stayed there. The ravens brought him bread and meat in the morning. They also brought him bread and meat in the evening. He drank water from the brook.

It was now three years since it had rained. A message came to Elijah from the LORD. He said, "Go. Speak to Ahab. Then I will send rain on the land."

So Elijah went to speak to Ahab.

There wasn't enough food in Samaria. The people there were very hungry.

When [Ahab] saw Elijah, he said to him, "Is that you? You are always stirring up trouble in Israel."

"I haven't made trouble for Israel," Elijah replied. "But you and your father's family have. You have turned away from the LORD's commands. You have followed the gods that are named after Baal.

"Now send for people from all over Israel. Tell them to meet me on Mount Carmel. And bring the 450 prophets of the god Baal. Also bring the 400 prophets of the goddess Asherah. All of them eat at Jezebel's table."

So Ahab sent that message all through Israel. He gathered the prophets together on Mount Carmel.

Elijah went there and stood in front of the people. He said, "How long will it take you to make up your minds? If the LORD is the one and only God, follow him. But if Baal is the one and only God, follow him."

The people didn't say anything.

Then Elijah said to them, "I'm the only one of the LORD's prophets left. But Baal has 450 prophets. Get two bulls for us. Let Baal's prophets choose one for themselves. Let them cut it into pieces. Then let them put it on the wood. But don't let them set fire to it. I'll prepare the other bull. I'll put it on the wood. But I won't set fire to it. Then you pray to your god. And I'll pray to the LORD. The god who answers by sending fire down is the one and only God."

Then all of the people said, "What you are saying is good."

The prophets of Baal prayed all day, but nothing happened. Then Elijah prayed to God, and God sent fire down from heaven that burned up the sacrifice, the wood, the stones, and the soil!

All of the people saw it. Then they fell down flat with their faces toward the ground. They cried out, "The LORD is the one and only God! The LORD is the one and only God!"

Then Elijah commanded them, "Grab hold of the prophets of Baal. Don't let a single one of them get away!"

So they grabbed them. Elijah had them brought down to the Kishon Valley. There he had them put to death.

Ahab told Jezebel everything Elijah had done. He told her how Elijah had killed all of the prophets with his sword.

So Jezebel sent a message to Elijah. She said, "You can be sure that I will kill you, just as I killed the other prophets. I'll do it by this time tomorrow. If I don't, may the gods punish me greatly."

Elijah was afraid. So he ran for his life. He came to Beersheba in Judah. He left his servant there.

Then he traveled for one day into the desert. He came to a small tree. He sat down under it. He prayed that he would die. "LORD, I've had enough," he said. "Take my life. I'm no better than my people of long ago." Then he lay down under the tree. And he fell asleep.

Suddenly an angel touched him. The angel said, "Get up and eat." Elijah looked around. Near his head he saw a flat cake of bread. It had been baked over hot coals. A jar of water was also there. So Elijah ate and drank. Then he lay down again.

The angel of the LORD came to him a second time. He touched him and said, "Get up and eat. Your journey will be long and hard."

So he got up. He ate and drank. The food gave him new

strength. He traveled for 40 days and 40 nights. He kept going until he arrived at Horeb. It was the mountain of God. There he went into a cave and spent the night.

A message came to Elijah from the LORD. He said, "Elijah, what are you doing here?"

He replied, "LORD God who rules over all, I've been very committed to you. The people of Israel have turned their backs on your covenant. They have torn down your altars. They've put your prophets to death with their swords. I'm the only one left. And they are trying to kill me."

The LORD said, "Go out. Stand on the mountain in front of me. I am going to pass by."

As the LORD approached, a very powerful wind tore the mountains apart. It broke up the rocks. But the LORD wasn't in the wind.

After the wind there was an earthquake. But the LORD wasn't in the earthquake.

After the earthquake a fire came. But the LORD wasn't in the fire.

And after the fire there was only a gentle whisper. When Elijah heard it, he pulled his coat over his face. He went out and stood at the entrance to the cave.

Then a voice said to him, "Elijah, what are you doing here?"

He replied, "LORD God who rules over all, I've been very committed to you. The people of Israel have turned their backs on your covenant. They have torn down your altars. They've put your prophets to death with their swords. I'm the only one left. And they are trying to kill me."

The LORD said to him, "Go back the way you came. Go to

the Desert of Damascus. When you get there, anoint Hazael as king over Aram. Also anoint Jehu as king over Israel.

"I will keep 7,000 people in Israel for myself. They have not bowed down to Baal. And they have not kissed him."

After God's message, Elijah went to find Elisha. When Elisha met Elijah, he left his life as a farmer and became Elijah's helper.

King Ahab went into war and died, and his son Ahaziah became king. Ahaziah was a wicked king like his father. When he died, his brother Joram became king.

Elijah was getting old, and God decided it was time for Elisha to become the main prophet in Israel. So Elijah and Elisha went on a journey to a place where God would do an amazing thing.

Elijah and Elisha were on their way from Gilgal. The LORD was going to use a strong wind to take Elijah up to heaven. Elijah said to Elisha, "Stay here. The LORD has sent me to Bethel."

But Elisha said, "I won't leave you. And that's just as sure as the LORD and you are alive." So they went down to Bethel.

Fifty men from the company of the prophets followed them. The men stopped and stood not far away from them. They faced the place where Elijah and Elisha had stopped at the Jordan River. Elijah rolled his coat up. Then he struck the water with it. The water parted to the right and to the left. The two of them went across the river on dry ground.

After they had gone across, Elijah spoke to Elisha. He said,

"Tell me. What can I do for you before I'm taken away from you?"

"Please give me a double share of your spirit," Elisha replied.

"You have asked me for something I can't give you," Elijah said. "Only the LORD can give it. But suppose you see me when I'm taken away from you. Then you will receive what you have asked for. If you don't see me, you won't receive it."

They kept walking along and talking together. Suddenly a chariot and horses appeared. Fire was all around them. The chariot and horses came between the two men. Then Elijah went up to heaven in a strong wind.

Elisha saw it. He cried out to Elijah, "My father! You are like a father to me! You are the true chariots and horsemen of Israel!"

Elisha didn't see Elijah anymore. Then Elisha took hold of his own clothes and tore them apart.

He picked up the coat that had fallen from Elijah. He went back and stood on the bank of the Jordan River. Then he struck the water with Elijah's coat. "Where is the power of the LORD?" he asked. "Where is the power of the God of Elijah?" When Elisha struck the water, it parted to the right and to the left. He went across the river.

The company of the prophets from Jericho were watching. They said, "The spirit of Elijah has been given to Elisha." They went over to him. They bowed down to him with their faces toward the ground.

God was with Elisha and he did many miraculous things. He brought a child back to life and healed a man without even touching him. After Elisha died, his bones brought a man back to life.

While Elijah and Elisha were prophets, Israel was a rich nation filled with sinful people. God kept getting angrier and angrier at the people's sin, because the people had forgotten that God, not the idols, had made them wealthy. But the people didn't care about God. God decided that if the people didn't repent, he would send kings from other countries to take away everything in Israel. God hoped the people would remember him. He sent a man named Amos to warn the people about what would happen if they kept worshiping idols. Amos said:

People of Israel, listen to the LORD's message. It is against you. It is against the whole family he brought up out of Egypt. He says,

"Out of all of the families on earth
    I have chosen only you.
So I will punish you
    because you have committed so many sins."

Speak to the people in the forts of Ashdod and Egypt.
    Tell them, "Gather together
    on the mountains of Samaria.
Look at the great trouble in that city.
    Its people are committing many crimes."

"They do not know how to do what is right,"
    announces the LORD.
    "They pile up stolen goods in their forts."

So the LORD and King says,

"Enemies will take over your land.
They will pull down your places of safety.
They will rob your forts."

The LORD and King has taken an oath
in his own holy name.
"I made sure your stomachs were empty in every city.
You did not have enough bread in any of your towns.
In spite of that, you still have not returned to me,"
announces the LORD.

"I sent plagues on you,
just as I did on Egypt.
I killed your young men with swords.
I also let the horses you had captured be killed.
I filled your noses with the bad smell of your camps.
In spite of that, you still have not returned to me,"
announces the LORD.
"People of Israel, I will punish you.
Because I will do that to you,
prepare to meet your God!"

Israel, look to the LORD and live.

Look to what is good, not to what is evil.
Then you will live.
And the LORD God who rules over all
will be with you,
just as you say he is.

Hate what is evil. Love what is good.
  Do what is fair in the courts.
Perhaps the LORD God who rules over all
  will show you his favor.
After all, you are the only ones left
  in the family line of Joseph.

"I am the LORD and King.
  My eyes are watching the sinful kingdom of Israel.
I will wipe it off the face of the earth.
  But I will not totally destroy the people of Jacob,"
    announces the LORD.

Even though God warned the people several times through his prophets Amos and Hosea, the people in Israel kept sinning. The people didn't follow God's rules or listen to God's warnings, so he carried out his punishment. Kings came and stole the money, destroyed all the houses and cities, and took the people away from Israel to live in other countries. The great nation of Israel was completely destroyed.

The kingdom of Judah continued. Some kings of Judah were good kings. They loved God and reminded the people of all that God had done for them. But many kings were very evil and allowed the people to worship idols. God sent prophets to the people in Judah to remind them that there was (and is) only one true God.

God sent another prophet, named Isaiah, to tell the people to repent. If they didn't, a powerful king would come to destroy the nation of Judah. He would steal the money, burn the land, and take the people far away. But because God had loved King David and promised that David's kingdom in Judah would never end, God wasn't going to completely destroy Judah like he had destroyed Israel. Isaiah's message told about horrible things that would happen, but it was also filled with hope for the future.

Discussion Questions

1. Have you ever talked with anyone about your faith in God? What made you choose that person?
2. Have you ever gone on a long journey?

   If so, where did you go?

   If you have never gone on a long journey, where would you like to go? Why?
3. Do you always say you're sorry when you hurt someone's feelings? Think about a time when someone hurt your feelings. Did you receive an apology? How did that make you feel?

16

The Beginning of the End

Isaiah gave the people his messages from God. If Judah changed and started obeying God, God would forgive them and protect them from the powerful, foreign kings. Isaiah's message was not pleasant. His news was difficult to think about or listen to. Would the people listen and ask for forgiveness? Isaiah said:

Here is what
    the LORD who rules over all is about to do.
The Lord will take away from Jerusalem and Judah
    supplies and help alike.
He will take away all of the supplies of food and water.
    He'll take away heroes and soldiers.

He'll take away judges and prophets.
He'll take away fortune tellers and elders.
He'll take away captains of companies of 50 men.
He'll take away government leaders.
He'll take away advisers, skilled workers
and those who are clever at doing evil magic.

The LORD will make young boys rule over all of them.
Mere children will govern them.
People will crush one another.
They will fight against each other.
They will fight against their neighbors.
Young people will attack old people.
Ordinary people will attack those who are more important.
Jerusalem is about to fall.
And so is Judah.
They say and do things against the LORD.
They dare to disobey him to his very face.
The look on their faces is a witness against them.
They show off their sin, just as the people of Sodom did.
They don't even try to hide it.
How terrible it will be for them!
They have brought trouble on themselves.

My people, your leaders have taken you down the wrong path.
They have turned you away from the right path.

The LORD takes his place in court.
    He stands up to judge the people.

Isaiah's message is one of the most amazing in the entire Bible. He tells of cities falling apart and the people of Judah being marched off in chains to a country called Babylon. But most of Isaiah's message was about what would happen in the future after the sadness and destruction. Here is more of what Isaiah said:

The LORD will show tender love toward Jacob's people.
    Once again he will choose Israel.
    He'll settle them in their own land.
Outsiders will join them.
    They and the people of Jacob will become one people.
Nations will help Israel
    return to their own land.
People from other nations will belong to Israel.
    They will serve them as male and female servants in the LORD's land.
The Israelites will make prisoners of those who had held them as prisoners.
    They will rule over those who had crushed them.

The LORD will put an end to Israel's suffering and trouble. They won't be slaves anymore. They will make fun of the king of Babylonia. They will say,

"See how the one who crushed others has fallen!
    See how his anger has come to an end!"
The LORD has taken away the authority of evil people.
    He has broken the power of rulers.

The LORD says to his servant,

"When it is time to show you my favor, I will answer your
prayers.
When it is time to save you, I will help you.
I will keep you safe.
You will put my covenant with the people of Israel
into effect.
Then their land will be made like new again.
Each tribe will be sent back to its territory that was
left empty.
I want you to say to the prisoners, 'Come out.'
Tell those who are in their dark cells, 'You are
free!'..."

Isaiah's message gets even better. Isaiah trusted God, and God let him see a lot of things that would happen in the future—a long way into the future. Isaiah talked about the Messiah, the person who would save all of Judah and the world from destruction and pain forever.

God shared this news about the Messiah hundreds of years before he was even born because he wanted the Jews (all the people from Judah) to know it would happen, and to look forward to it with hope.

Who has believed what we've been saying?
  Who has seen the LORD's saving power?
His servant grew up like a tender young plant.
  He grew like a root coming up out of dry ground.
He didn't have any beauty or majesty that made us notice him.
  There wasn't anything special about the way he looked that drew us to him.
Men looked down on him. They didn't accept him.
  He knew all about sorrow and suffering.
He was like someone people turn their faces away from.
  We looked down on him. We didn't have any respect for him.

He suffered the things we should have suffered.
  He took on himself the pain that should have been ours.
But we thought God was punishing him.
  We thought God was wounding him and making him suffer.
But the servant was pierced because we had sinned.
  He was crushed because we had done what was evil.
He was punished to make us whole again.
  His wounds have healed us.
All of us are like sheep. We have wandered away from God.
  All of us have turned to our own way.

And the LORD has placed on his servant
    the sins of all of us.

He was beaten down and made to suffer.
    But he didn't open his mouth.
He was led away like a sheep to be killed.
    Lambs are silent while their wool is being cut off.
    In the same way, he didn't open his mouth.
He was arrested and sentenced to death.
    Then he was taken away.
    He was cut off from this life.
He was punished for the sins of my people.
    Who among those who were living at that time
    could have understood those things?
He was given a grave with those who were evil.
    But his body was buried in the tomb of a rich man.
He was killed even though he hadn't harmed anyone.
    And he had never lied to anyone.

The LORD says, "It was my plan to crush him
    and cause him to suffer.
    I made his life a guilt offering to pay for sin.
But he will see all of his children after him.
    In fact, he will continue to live.
    My plan will be brought about through him.
After he suffers, he will see the light that leads to
        life.
    And he will be satisfied.
My godly servant will make many people godly
    because of what he will accomplish.
    He will be punished for their sins.

So I will give him a place of honor among those who are
great.
He will be rewarded just like others who win the
battle.
That is because he was willing to give his life as a
sacrifice.
He was counted among those who had committed
crimes.
He took the sins of many people on himself.
And he gave his life for those who had done what is
wrong."

Discussion Questions

1. If you ruled a country, what kind of ruler would you be? What rules would you make for your people?
2. What is the last thing you prayed for?
3. God answers all of our prayers, even if sometimes the answer is to wait. What can you do while you are waiting for an answer?

17

The Kingdoms' Fall

Unfortunately, the people in Judah didn't listen to Isaiah. God called another prophet, named Jeremiah, to warn all the people yet again that the king of Babylon would destroy everything and take the people off as slaves. God chose Jeremiah for this special assignment. Jeremiah said:

A message came to me from the LORD. He said,

"Before I formed you in your mother's body I chose you.
Before you were born I set you apart to serve me.
I appointed you to be a prophet to the nations."

"You are my LORD and King," I said. "I don't know how to speak. I'm only a child."

But the LORD said to me, "Do not say, 'I'm only a child.' You must go to everyone I send you to. You must say everything I command you to say. Do not be afraid of the people I send you to. I am with you. I will save you," announces the LORD.

Then the LORD reached out his hand. He touched my mouth and spoke to me. He said, "I have put my words in your mouth. Today I am appointing you to speak to nations and kingdoms. I want you to pull them up by the roots and tear them down. I want you to destroy them and crush them. But I also want you to build them up and plant them."

Jeremiah was scared by what God wanted him to do because he knew the kings of Judah were hard headed and wouldn't like his message. But he trusted God, and he knew his message was important to the people in Jerusalem. Jeremiah told the people, "This is what the LORD says:

"You were like a good vine when I planted you.
    You were a healthy plant.
Then how did you turn against me?
    How did you become a bad, wild vine?
You might wash yourself with baking soda.
    You might use plenty of soap.
    But I can still see the stains your guilt covers you
        with,"
                announces the LORD and King.

"A thief is dishonored when he is caught.
    And you people of Israel are filled with shame.
Your kings and officials are dishonored.
    So are your priests and your prophets.

You say to a piece of wood, 'You are my father.'
You say to a stone, 'You are my mother.'
You have turned your backs to me.
You refuse to look at me.
But when you are in trouble, you say,
'Come and save us!'
So where are the gods you made for yourselves?
Let them come when you are in trouble!
Let them save you if they can!
Judah, you have as many gods as you have towns."

The LORD says, "Go up and down the streets of Jerusalem.
Look around.
Think about what you see.
Search through the market places.
See if you can find one honest person who tries to be truthful.
If you can, I will forgive this city."

If you don't listen,
I will sob in secret.
Because you are so proud,
I will sob bitterly.
Tears will flow from my eyes.
The LORD's flock will be taken away as prisoners.
Speak to the king and his mother. Tell them,
"Come down from your thrones.
Your glorious crowns
are about to fall from your heads."

The gates of the cities in the Negev Desert will be shut
tight.
There won't be anyone to open them.
You will be carried away as prisoners.
You will be taken away completely.

Jeremiah told the people over and over about the horrible things that would happen if they didn't repent, but no one listened. One king burned Jeremiah's prophecies because he thought they were not true. The kings of Judah were so sure nothing would happen; they did things that made the leaders of Babylon angry.

So Nebuchadnezzar, the king of Babylon, attacked Judah and took some of the smartest and strongest people away to Babylon. But not even this attack made the people listen to Jeremiah's message.

The LORD, the God of Israel, sent word to his people through his messengers. He sent it to them again and again. He took pity on his people. He also took pity on the temple where he lived.

But God's people made fun of his messengers. They hated his words. They laughed at his prophets. Finally the LORD's burning anger was stirred up against his people. Nothing could save them.

Zedekiah was 21 years old when he became king. He ruled in Jerusalem for 11 years.

He did what was evil in the sight of the LORD his God. He didn't pay any attention to the message the LORD spoke through the prophet Jeremiah.

Zedekiah also refused to remain under the control of King Nebuchadnezzar. The king had made him take an oath in God's name. But his heart became very stubborn. He wouldn't turn to the LORD, the God of Israel.

And that's not all. The people and the leaders of the priests became more and more unfaithful. They followed all of the practices of the nations. The LORD hated those practices. The people and leaders made the LORD's temple "unclean." The LORD had set the temple in Jerusalem apart in a special way for himself.

Nebuchadnezzar was king of Babylonia. He marched out against Jerusalem. All of his armies went with him. It was in the ninth year of the rule of Zedekiah. It was on the tenth day of the tenth month. Nebuchadnezzar set up camp outside the city. He brought in war machines all around it. It was surrounded until the 11th year of King Zedekiah's rule.

By the ninth day of the fourth month, there wasn't any food left in the city. So the people didn't have anything to eat.

Then the Babylonians broke through the city wall. Judah's whole army ran away at night. They went out through the gate between the two walls that were near the king's garden. They escaped even though the Babylonians surrounded the city. Judah's army ran toward the Arabah Valley.

But the armies of Babylonia chased King Zedekiah. They caught up with him in the flatlands near Jericho. All of his soldiers were separated from him. They had scattered in every direction.

The king was captured. He was taken to the king of Babylonia at Riblah. That's where Nebuchadnezzar decided how he would be punished ... They put him in bronze chains. And they took him to Babylon.

Some people still remained in the city. But the commander Nebuzaradan took them away as prisoners. He also took the rest of the people of the land. That included those who had joined the king of Babylonia.

But the commander left some of the poorest people of the land behind. He told them to work in the vineyards and fields.

Jeremiah had trusted God and done what God wanted—even when it got him in trouble with the king—so God promised to protect Jeremiah. When a powerful leader from Babylon found Jeremiah, he let Jeremiah go and promised to take care of him.

Someone (many people believe it was Jeremiah himself) wrote sad poetry about Judah, called Lamentations. He was sad to see his homeland destroyed and all the people taken away. This is what was written:

The city of Jerusalem is so empty!
  It used to be full of people.
But now it's like a woman whose husband has died.
  She used to be great among the nations.
She was like a queen among the kingdoms.
  But now she is a slave.

The LORD has done what he planned to do.
  He has made what he said come true.
  He gave the command long ago.

He has destroyed you without pity.
He has let your enemies laugh at you.
He has made them stronger than you are.

But here is something else I remember.
And it gives me hope.
The LORD loves us very much.
So we haven't been completely destroyed.
His loving concern never fails.
His great love is new every morning.
LORD, how faithful you are!
I say to myself, "The LORD is everything I will ever need.
So I will put my hope in him."
The LORD is good to those who put their hope in him.
He is good to those who look to him.
It is good when people wait quietly
for the LORD to save them.

LORD, think about what has happened to us.
  Look at the shame our enemies have brought on us.
There isn't any joy in our hearts.
  Our dancing has turned into sobbing.
All of our honor is gone.
  How terrible it is for us! We have sinned.

LORD, you rule forever.
  Your throne will last for all time to come.
Why do you always forget us?
  Why have you deserted us for so long?
LORD, please bring us back to you.
  Then we can return.
  Make our lives like new again.

While Jeremiah was prophesying in Judah, God used a man named Ezekiel to talk to the people. Ezekiel lived in Babylon and spoke to God's people who had been captured. He reminded the people that God was still watching over them, even in Babylon.

I was 30 years old. I was with my people who had been taken away from their country. We were by the Kebar River in the land of Babylonia. On the fifth day of the fourth month, the heavens were opened. I saw visions of God.

I looked up and saw a windstorm coming from the north. I saw a huge cloud. The fire of lightning was flashing out of it. Bright light surrounded it. The center of the fire looked like glowing metal.

I saw in the fire something that looked like four living creatures. They appeared to have the shape of a man. But each of them had four faces and four wings.

Something that looked like a huge space was spread out above the heads of the living creatures. It gleamed like ice. It was terrifying. The wings of the creatures were spread out under the space. They reached out toward one another. Each creature had two wings covering its body.

When the creatures moved, I heard the sound of their wings. It was like the roar of rushing waters. It sounded like the thundering voice of the Mighty One. It was like the loud noise an army makes. When the creatures stood still, they lowered their wings.

Then a voice came from above the huge space over their heads. They stood with their wings lowered. Above the space over their heads was something that looked like a throne made out of sapphire.

On the throne high above was a figure that appeared to be human. From his waist up he looked like glowing metal that was full of fire. From his waist down he looked like fire. Bright light surrounded him. The glow around him looked like a rainbow in the clouds on a rainy day.

That's what the glory of the Lord looked like. When I saw it, I fell with my face toward the ground. Then I heard the voice of someone speaking.

He said to me, "Son of man, stand up on your feet. I will speak to you." As he spoke, the Spirit of the Lord came into me. He raised me to my feet. I heard him speaking to me.

He said, "Son of man, I am sending you to the people of Israel. That nation has refused to obey me. They have turned against me. They and their people before them have been against me to this very day. The people I am sending you to are very stubborn. Tell them, 'Here is what the LORD and King says.'

"Son of man, do not be afraid of them or of what they say. Do not be afraid, even if thorns and bushes are all around you and you live among scorpions. Do not be afraid of what they say. Do not be terrified by them. They always refuse to obey me.

"You must give them my message. They might listen, or they might not. After all, they refuse to obey me."

Ezekiel did some strange things to show the people what was happening back in Judah. His actions made the people listen to him, and once he had everyone's attention, he gave them a very important message: God was going to let the people go back to Judah some day. In fact, he was going to completely forgive them and make them a stronger nation than they ever were before. Here's what God told Ezekiel:

"Tell the people of Israel, 'The LORD and King speaks. He says, "People of Israel, I will not take action for your benefit. Instead, I will act for the honor of my holy name. You have treated it as if it were not holy. You did it everywhere you went among the nations. But I will show everyone how holy my great name is. You have treated it as if it were not holy. So I will use you to show the nations how holy I am. Then they will know that I am the LORD," announces the LORD and King.

" ' "I will take you out of the nations. I will gather you together from all of the countries. I will bring you back into your own land.

" ' "I will sprinkle pure water on you. Then you will be 'clean.' I will make you completely pure and clean. I will take all of the statues of your gods away from you. I will give you new hearts. I will give you a new spirit that is faithful to me. I will remove your stubborn hearts from you. I will give you hearts that obey me.

" ' "I will put my Spirit in you. I will move you to follow my rules. I want you to be careful to keep my laws. You will live in the land I gave your people long ago. You will be my people. And I will be your God." ' "

The LORD and King says, "I will make you pure from all of your sins. On that day I will settle you in your towns again. Your broken-down houses will be rebuilt. The dry and empty land will be farmed again.

"Everyone who passes through it will see that it is no longer empty. They will say, 'This land was completely destroyed. But now it's like the Garden of Eden. The cities were full of broken-down buildings. They were destroyed and empty. But now they have high walls around them. And people live in them.'

"Then the nations that remain around you will know that I have rebuilt what was once destroyed. I have planted again the fields that were once empty. I have spoken. And I will do it. I am the LORD."

Discussion Questions

1. Have you ever stolen something from someone? If so, did you give it back? Did you apologize? Has anyone ever stolen from you?
2. Have you or one of your friends ever been picked on by other kids? How did it make you feel? How did you handle the situation?
3. Why should we pray for people (even those who do mean things)?

18

God Watches Over Daniel

The Jews lived in Babylon for a long time under Babylonian kings. Eventually another kingdom, called Persia, took over Babylon, and Darius became king.

It pleased Darius to appoint 120 royal rulers over his entire kingdom. He placed three leaders over them. One of the leaders was Daniel. The royal rulers were made accountable to the three leaders. Then the king wouldn't lose any of his wealth. Daniel did a better job than the other two leaders or any of the royal rulers. He was an unusually good and able man. So the king planned to put him in charge of the whole kingdom.

But the other two leaders and the royal rulers heard about it. So they looked for a reason to bring charges against

Daniel. They tried to find something wrong with the way he ran the government. But they weren't able to. They couldn't find any fault with his work. He could always be trusted. He never did anything wrong. And he always did what he was supposed to.

Finally those men said, "It's almost impossible for us to come up with a reason to bring charges against this man Daniel. If we do, it will have to be in connection with the law of his God."

So the two leaders and the royal rulers went as a group to the king. They said, "King Darius, may you live forever! All of the royal leaders, high officials, royal rulers, advisers and governors want to make a suggestion. We've agreed that you should give an order. And you should make sure it's obeyed. Here is the command you should give. King Darius, during the next 30 days don't let any of your people pray to any god or man except to you. If they do, throw them into the lions' den.

"Now give the order. Write it down in the laws of the Medes and Persians. Then it can't be changed." So King Darius put the order in writing.

Daniel found out that the king had signed the order. In spite of that, he did just as he had always done before. He went home to his upstairs room. Its windows opened toward Jerusalem. He went to his room three times a day to pray. He got down on his knees and gave thanks to his God.

Some of the other royal officials went to where Daniel was staying. They saw him praying and asking God for help. So they went to the king. They spoke to him about his royal order. They said, "King Darius, didn't you sign an official order? It said that for the next 30 days none of your people could pray to any god or man except to you. If they did, they would be thrown into the lions' den."

The king answered, "The order must still be obeyed. It's one of the laws of the Medes and Persians. So it can't be changed."

Then they spoke to the king again. They said, "Daniel is one of the prisoners from Judah. He doesn't pay any attention to you, King Darius. He doesn't obey the order you put into writing. He still prays to his God three times a day."

When the king heard that, he was very upset. He didn't want Daniel to be harmed in any way. Until sunset, he did everything he could to save him.

Then the men went as a group to the king. They said to him, "King Darius, remember that no order or law you make can be changed. That's what the laws of the Medes and Persians require."

So the king gave the order. Daniel was brought out and thrown into the lions' den. The king said to him, "You always serve your God faithfully. So may he save you!"

A stone was brought and placed over the opening of the den. The king sealed it with his own special ring. He also sealed it with the rings of his nobles. Then nothing could be done to help Daniel.

The king returned to his palace. He didn't eat anything that night. He didn't ask for anything to be brought to him for his enjoyment. And he couldn't sleep.

As soon as the sun began to rise, the king got up. He hurried to the lions' den. When he got near it, he called out to Daniel. His voice was filled with great concern. He said, "Daniel! You serve the living God. You always serve him faithfully. So has he been able to save you from the lions?"

Daniel answered, "My king, may you live forever! My God sent his angel. And his angel shut the mouths of the lions. They haven't hurt me at all. That's because I haven't done anything wrong in God's sight. I've never done anything wrong to you either, my king."

The king was filled with joy. He ordered his servants to lift Daniel out of the den. So they did. They didn't see any wounds on him. That's because he had trusted in his God.

Daniel, who had been captured in Judah by the Babylonians, remembered Jeremiah's messages which said that one day God would bring his people back to Judah. While the people were in exile, they talked about Jeremiah's words as they waited for God to rescue them. Imagine their hope when they read what the Lord had told Jeremiah to write:

"I am the LORD. I am the God of Israel. I say, 'Write on a scroll all of the words I have spoken to you. A new day is coming,' " announces the LORD. " 'At that time I will bring my people Israel and Judah back from where they have been taken as prisoners. I will bring them back to this land. Long ago I gave it to their people to have as their own,' " says the LORD.

" 'At that time I will break the yoke off their necks,'
announces the LORD who rules over all.
'I will tear off the ropes that hold them.
People from other lands will not make them slaves
anymore.' "

" 'People of Jacob, do not be afraid.
You are my servant.
Israel, do not be terrified,' "
announces the LORD.
" 'You can be sure that I will save you.
I will bring you out of a place far away.
I will bring your children back
from the land where they were taken.

Your people will have peace and security again.
And no one will make them afraid.
I am with you. I will save you,' "
announces the LORD.
" 'I will completely destroy all of the nations
among which I scatter you.
But I will not completely destroy you.
I will correct you. But I will be fair.
I will punish you in a way that is fair and right.' "

The LORD who rules over all is the God of Israel. He says, "I will bring them back from the place where they were taken. The people in Judah and its towns will say once again, 'Holy temple in Jerusalem, may the LORD bless you. Sacred mountain, may he bless you.'

"People will live together in Judah and all of its towns. Farmers and shepherds will live there. I will give rest to those who are tired. I will satisfy those who are weak."

The LORD says, "You will be forced to live in Babylonia for 70 years. After they are over, I will come to you. My gracious promise to you will come true. I will bring you back home.

"I know the plans I have for you," announces the LORD. "I want you to enjoy success. I do not plan to harm you. I will give you hope for the years to come. Then you will call out to me. You will come and pray to me. And I will listen to you. When you look for me with all your heart, you will find me.

"I will be found by you," announces the LORD. "And I will bring you back from where you were taken as prisoners. I will gather you from all of the nations. I will gather you from the places where I have forced you to go," announces the LORD. "I will bring you back to the place from which I sent you away."

As the people waited for the day when they could go home and be free again, God started doing some wonderful things to shorten the wait. Cyrus, the king of Persia, knew who God was, so he was nice to God's people. God told Cyrus to let some of the people go back to Judah to clean up the rubble and dust and make it a home again.

Discussion Questions

1. Have you ever been the new kid at school or in a group of some kind? What did you do to get used to the surroundings and people?
2. Has anyone ever made fun of you for going to church or praying? What did you do?
3. Have you ever been scared and asked God to watch over you? What were you afraid of? Did praying make you feel less afraid?

19

The Return Home

It was the first year of the rule of Cyrus. He was king of Persia. The LORD stirred him up to send a message all through his kingdom. It happened so that what the LORD had spoken through Jeremiah would come true. The message was written down. It said,

"Cyrus, the king of Persia, says,

" 'The LORD is the God of heaven. He has given me all of the kingdoms on earth. He has appointed me to build a temple for him at Jerusalem in Judah.

" 'Any one of his people among you can go up to Jerusalem. And may your God be with you. You can build the LORD's temple. He is the God of Israel. He is the God who is in Jerusalem.

" 'The people who are still left alive in every place must bring him gifts. They must provide him with silver and gold.

They must bring goods and livestock. They should also bring any offerings they choose to. All of those gifts will be for God's temple in Jerusalem.'"

Then everyone God had stirred up got ready to go. They wanted to go up to Jerusalem and build the LORD's temple there. They included the family leaders of Judah and Benjamin. They also included the priests and Levites.

All of their neighbors helped them. They gave them silver and gold articles. They gave them goods and livestock. And they gave them gifts of great value. All of those things were added to the other offerings the people chose to give.

King Cyrus also brought out the articles that belonged to the LORD's temple. Nebuchadnezzar had carried them off from Jerusalem. He had put them in the temple of his own god.

A priest named Jeshua and a leader named Zerubbabel led over 42,000 people back to Judah. The people were eager to return to Jerusalem, even though their homes had been ruined and needed to be rebuilt. There was a lot to do, but first the people wanted to rebuild the temple. The temple was very important because it meant God would be with the people again. It would also give them a place to show God how happy they were to be home.

The builders laid the foundation of the LORD's temple. Then the priests came. They were wearing their special clothes. They brought their trumpets with them. The Levites who belonged to the family line of Asaph also came. They brought their cymbals with them. The priests and Levites took their places to praise the LORD. They did everything just as King David had required them to. They sang to the LORD. They praised him. They gave thanks to him. They said,

"The LORD is good.
His faithful love to Israel continues forever."

All of the people gave a loud shout. They praised the LORD. They were glad because the foundation of the LORD's temple had been laid.

But many of the older priests and Levites and family leaders sobbed out loud. They had seen the first temple. So when they saw the foundation of the second temple being laid, they sobbed. Others shouted with joy.

No one could tell the difference between the shouts of joy and the sounds of sobbing. That's because the people made so much noise. The sound was heard far away.

Then the nations that were around Judah tried to make its people lose hope. They wanted to make them afraid to go on building. So they hired advisers to work against them. They wanted their plans to fail. They did it during the whole time Cyrus was king of Persia. They kept doing it until Darius became king.

And so the work on the house of God in Jerusalem came to an end. Nothing more was done on it until the second year that Darius was king of Persia.

God knew building the temple was very important. So he sent Haggai, another prophet, to tell the people to start working on the temple again. Haggai said:

The LORD who rules over all says, "The people of Judah are saying, 'The time hasn't come yet for the LORD's temple to be rebuilt.' "

So the message came to me from the LORD. He said, "My temple is still destroyed. In spite of that, you are living in your houses that have beautiful wooden walls."

The LORD who rules over all says, "Think carefully about how you are living. You have planted many seeds. But the crops you have gathered are small. So you eat. But you never have enough. You drink. But you are never full. You put your clothes on. But you are not warm. You earn your pay. But it will not buy everything you need."

He continues, "Think carefully about how you are living. Go up into the mountains. Bring logs down. Use them to rebuild my house. Then I will enjoy it. And you will honor me," says the LORD.

"You expected a lot. But you can see what a small amount it turned out to be," announces the LORD who rules over all. "I blew away what you brought home. Why? Because my temple is still destroyed. In spite of that, each one of you is busy with your own house.

"So because of what you have done, the heavens have held back the dew. And the earth has not produced its crops. I ordered the rain not to fall on the fields and mountains. Then the ground did not produce any grain. There were not enough grapes to make fresh wine. The trees did not bear enough olives to make oil. People and cattle suffered. All of your hard work failed."

Haggai gave the message to men who loved God.
The men decided to help build the temple right away.

The temple they had to build was to be as big and gold-plated and magnificent as the one Solomon built years and years ago. God wanted things exactly the way they used to be when Judah loved him.

God sent another prophet named Zechariah to tell the people what the temple needed to be like and to encourage them to work hard. He also reminded them that God would always love them. God told Zechariah to tell the people:

"I am very jealous for my people in Zion. In fact, I am burning with jealousy for them.

He continued, "I will return to Zion. I will live among my people in Jerusalem. Then Jerusalem will be called The City of Truth. And my mountain will be called The Holy Mountain."

He continued, "Once again old men and women will sit in the streets of Jerusalem. All of them will be using canes because they are old. The city streets will be filled with boys and girls. They will be playing there.

"All of that might seem wonderful to the people who are living at that time. But it will not seem wonderful to me."

He continued, "I will save my people. I will gather them from the countries of the east and the west. I will bring them back to live in Jerusalem. They will be my people. I will be their faithful God. I will keep my promises to them."

The Lord who rules over all says to his people, "Listen to the words that were spoken by the prophets Haggai and Zechariah. They spoke to you when the work on my temple started up again. Let your hands be strong so that you can rebuild the temple.

"Before the work was started again, there was no pay for the people or food for the animals. People could not go about their business safely because of their enemies. I had turned all of them against one another. But now I will not punish you who are living at this time. I will not treat you as I treated your people before you," announces the LORD who rules over all.

"Your seeds will grow well. Your vines will bear fruit. The ground will produce crops for you. And the heavens will drop their dew on your land. I will give all of those things to those who are still left alive here.

"Judah and Israel, in the past the nations called down curses on you. But now I will save you. You will be a blessing to others. Do not be afraid. Let your hands be strong so that you can do my work.

"Here is what you must do. Speak the truth to one another. Make true and wise decisions in your courts. Do not make evil plans against your neighbors. When you take an oath to tell the truth, do not lie. Many people love to do that. But I hate all of those things," announces the LORD.

He continued, "Many nations will still come to you. And those who live in many cities will also come. The people who live in one city will go to another city. They will say, 'Let's go right away to ask the LORD to show us his favor. Let's look to him as our God. We ourselves are going.' Large numbers of people and nations will come to Jerusalem. They will look to me. They will ask me to show them my favor."

Building the temple was hard work. Many of the people who lived in Judah while the people were in exile didn't want the Jews building the temple. They bothered the workers and wrote letters to King Darius to stop the Jews from building. The Jews told their enemies that Cyrus had sent them. They told the people what he had given them before they left Babylon.

"King Cyrus gave an order to rebuild this house of God. He gave it in the first year he was king of Babylonia. He even removed some gold and silver articles from the temple of Babylon. Nebuchadnezzar had brought them there from the house of God in Jerusalem. He had taken them to the temple in Babylon.

"Then King Cyrus brought them out. He gave them to a man named Sheshbazzar. Cyrus had appointed him as governor. He told him, 'Take these articles with you. Go and put them in the temple in Jerusalem. Rebuild the house of God in the same place where it stood before.'

"So Sheshbazzar made the trip to Jerusalem. He laid the foundations of the house of God there. From that day until now the people have been working on it. But they haven't finished it yet."

If it pleases you, King Darius, let a search be made in the official records of the kings of Babylonia. Find out whether King Cyrus really did give an order to rebuild this house of God in Jerusalem. Then tell us what you decide to do.

Darius looked through the old letters in the kingdom and found Cyrus's letter about the Jews and the temple. The Jews were right—they had permission to build the temple. Darius told the trouble makers to leave the Jews alone.

The elders of the Jews continued to build the temple. They enjoyed great success because of the preaching of the prophets Haggai and Zechariah …

The people finished building the temple. That's what the God of Israel had commanded them to do.

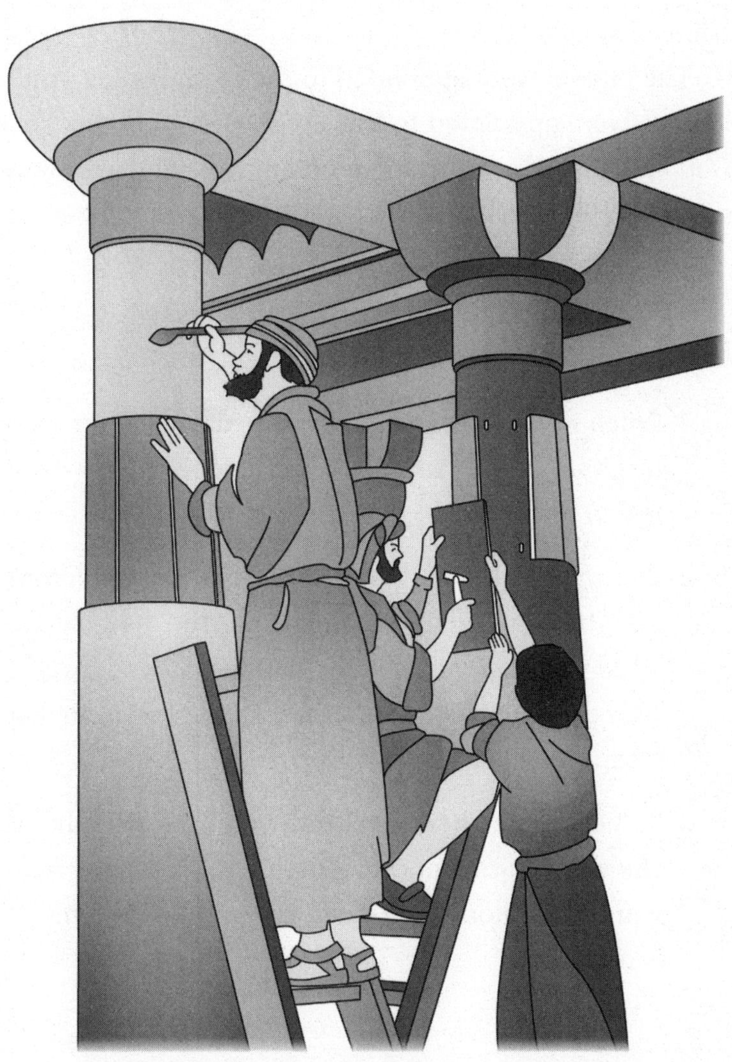

When the house of God was set apart, the people of Israel celebrated with joy. The priests and Levites joined them. So did the rest of those who had returned from Babylonia. When the house of God was set apart to him, the people sacrificed 100 bulls. They also sacrificed 200 rams and 400 male lambs. As a sin offering for the whole nation of Israel, the people sacrificed 12 male goats. One goat was sacrificed for each tribe in Israel.

The priests were appointed to their companies. And the Levites were appointed to their groups. All of them served God at Jerusalem. They served him in keeping with what is written in the Scroll of Moses.

Discussion Questions

1. When was the last time you helped a neighbor (or a neighbor helped you)? How did you help? How did it feel to be helped?
2. When was the last time you were disappointed? (Maybe your team lost a game, the new movie wasn't that great, or your teacher moved away?) How can you use your faith to gain comfort from that disappointment?
3. If one of your friends asked if you liked what he or she was wearing and you didn't like it, what would you say (without lying)? Is there ever a time when it is okay to lie?

20

The Queen of Beauty and Courage

King Xerxes became king of Persia. He wanted a new wife to be his queen. Officials in every part of the kingdom brought young women to the palace to see who Xerxes would like best.

A man named Mordecai lived near the palace with his cousin, Esther. (Esther's parents had died, so Mordecai took care of her.) Because she was so beautiful, Esther was taken to the palace and given special beauty treatments and food so she would look really nice for the king.

Esther was well liked by the servants in the palace, but she had a secret—she was Jewish.

Esther hadn't told anyone who her people were. She hadn't talked about her family. That's because Mordecai had told her not to.

Mordecai tried to find out how Esther was getting along. He wanted to know what was happening to her. So he walked back and forth near the courtyard by the place where the [women] stayed. He did it every day.

Each [woman] had to complete 12 months of beauty care. They used oil of myrrh for six months. And they used perfume and make-up for the other six months. A [woman's] turn to go in to King Xerxes could come only after a full 12 months had passed.

[Esther] was taken to King Xerxes in the royal house.

The king liked Esther more than he liked any of the other women ... So he put a royal crown on her head. He made her queen.

Then the king gave a big dinner. It was in honor of Esther. All of his nobles and officials were invited. He announced a holiday all through the territories he ruled over. He freely gave many gifts in keeping with his royal wealth.

The king had an official named Haman who was more powerful than anyone else in the kingdom, except the king. Haman liked having power. If anyone didn't do what he wanted, he would punish them.

The king gave Haman a higher position than he had before. He gave him a seat of honor. It was higher than the positions any of the other nobles had. All of the royal officials at the palace gate got down on their knees. They gave honor to Haman. That's because the king had commanded them to do it.

But Mordecai refused to get down on his knees. He wouldn't give Haman any honor at all.

The royal officials at the palace gate asked Mordecai a question. They said, "Why don't you obey the king's command?" Day after day they spoke to him. But he still refused to obey. So they told Haman about it. They wanted to see whether he would let Mordecai get away with what he was doing. Mordecai had told them he was a Jew.

Haman noticed that Mordecai wouldn't get down on his knees. He wouldn't give Haman any honor. So Haman burned with anger. But he had found out who Mordecai's people were. So he decided not to kill just Mordecai. He also looked for a way to destroy all of Mordecai's people. They were Jews. He wanted to kill all of them everywhere in the kingdom of Xerxes.

Then Haman said to King Xerxes, "Certain people are scattered among the nations. They live in all of the territories in your kingdom. Their practices are different from the practices of all other people. They don't obey your laws. It really isn't good for you to put up with them.

"If it pleases you, give the order to destroy them."

The king said to Haman, "Do what you want to with those people."

The king sent for the royal secretaries ... The secretaries wrote down all of Haman's orders.

Haman was an evil man. Just because Mordacai wouldn't bow down to him, Haman was planning to kill all the Jews! King Xerxes made the law because he trusted Haman, and so orders went out that all the Jewish people would have to die.

Mordacai was very scared. He told Queen Esther what was going to happen to all the Jews. Because no one knew Esther was Jewish, and the king loved her very much, Mordacai wanted Esther to ask the king to stop the law so none of the Jews would die.

Now Esther was scared. People weren't supposed to tell the king what to do. What would Xerxes do to her if he got mad?

Esther put her royal robes on. She stood in the inner courtyard of the palace. It was in front of the king's hall.

The king was sitting on his royal throne in the hall. He was facing the entrance. He saw Queen Esther standing in the courtyard. He was pleased with her. So he reached out toward her the gold rod that was in his hand. Then Esther approached him. She touched the tip of the rod.

The king asked, "What is it, Queen Esther? What do you want? I'll give it to you. I'll even give you up to half of my kingdom."

Esther replied, "King Xerxes, if it pleases you, come to a big dinner today. I've prepared it for you. Please have Haman come with you."

"Bring Haman at once," the king said to his servants. "Then we'll do what Esther asks."

So the king and Haman went to the big dinner Esther had prepared ... The king asked Esther the same question again. He said, "What do you want? I'll give it to you. What do you want me to do for you? I'll even give you up to half of my kingdom."

Esther replied, "Here is what I want. Here is my appeal to you ... I hope you will be pleased to give me what I want. And I hope you will be pleased to listen to my appeal. If you are, I'd like you and Haman to come tomorrow to the big dinner I'll prepare for you. Then I'll answer your question."

The very next day...

The king and Haman went to dine with Queen Esther ... The king again asked, "What do you want, Queen Esther? I'll give it to you. What do you want me to do for you? I'll even give you up to half of my kingdom."

Then Queen Esther answered, "King Xerxes, I hope you will show me your favor. I hope you will be pleased to let me live. That's what I want. Please spare my people. That's my appeal to you.

"My people and I have been sold to be destroyed. We've been sold to be killed and wiped out. Suppose we had only been sold as male and female slaves. Then I wouldn't have

said anything. That kind of suffering wouldn't be a good enough reason to bother you."

King Xerxes asked Queen Esther, "Who is the man who has dared to do such a thing? And where is he?"

Esther said, "The man hates us! He's our enemy! He's this evil Haman!"

Then Haman was terrified in front of the king and queen.

Esther did it! She saved all the Jewish people from hateful Haman. The king punished Haman. When Xerxes found out that Mordecai was Esther's cousin, he gave him Haman's old job. God's people were kept safe.

Discussion Questions

1. If you could be a king or queen for one day, what are three things you would do?
2. When you see that someone is being left out, what can you do?
3. What do you think is the most amazing thing about God?

21

Rebuilding the Walls

About sixty years after the temple was finished in Jerusalem, the king of Persia said all the Jews could go back to Judah. One of these Jews was named Ezra, who was a priest. The king of Persia wanted him to help at the temple. He gave Ezra silver and gold and animals for sacrifices so the people could worship God right way.

After all of those things had happened, Ezra came up to Jerusalem from Babylonia. It was during the rule of Artaxerxes. He was king of Persia.

Some of the people of Israel came up to Jerusalem too. They included priests, Levites and singers. They also included the temple servants and those who guarded the temple gates. It was in the seventh year that Artaxerxes was king.

Ezra had committed himself to study and obey the Law of the Lord. He also wanted to teach the Lord's rules and laws in Israel.

Ezra was a priest and teacher. He was an educated man. He knew the Lord's commands and rules for Israel very well.

Some of God's people who helped rebuild Jerusalem married sinful people living in the area (and these people worshipped false gods). Ezra prayed to God for forgiveness. When the people saw what Ezra was doing, they were sorry and asked for forgiveness.

The people were doing what God wanted, but they weren't finished rebuilding the cities. When a man named Nehemiah heard that Jerusalem wasn't completely rebuilt yet, he was very upset. Because Nehemiah was a winetaster for the Persian king, he asked the king for permission to return to Judah to rebuild the walls of the city. Here's what Nehemiah wrote:

At that time Hanani came from Judah with some other men. He was one of my brothers. I asked him and the other men about the Jews who were left alive in Judah. They had returned from Babylonia. I also asked him about Jerusalem.

He and the men who were with him said to me, "Some of the people who returned are still alive. They are back in the land of Judah. But they are having a hard time. People are making fun of them. The wall of Jerusalem is broken down. Its gates have been burned with fire."

When I heard about those things, I sat down and sobbed. For several days I was very sad. I didn't eat any food. And I prayed to the God of heaven. I said,

"LORD, you are the God of heaven. You are a great and wonderful God. You keep the covenant you made with those who love you and obey your commands. You show them your love.

"Please pay careful attention to my prayer. See how your people are suffering. Please listen to me. I'm praying to you day and night. I'm praying for the people of Israel. We Israelites have committed sins against you. All of us admit it. I and my family have also sinned against you.

Lord, please pay careful attention to my prayer. Listen to the prayers of all of us.

God knew Nehemiah would help the people in Jerusalem, so he answered Nehemiah's prayer. Nehemiah soon was in charge of rebuilding the wall. He had a plan for getting things done, but things weren't always easy. Nehemiah said:

I prayed to God. I said, "Our God, please listen to our prayer. Some people hate us. They're making fun of us. So let others make fun of them. Let them be carried off like stolen goods. Let them be taken to another country as prisoners. Don't hide your eyes from their guilt. Don't forgive their sins. They have made fun of the builders."

So we rebuilt the wall. We repaired it until all of it was half as high as we wanted it to be. The people worked with all their heart.

The people worked hard and made a lot of progress on the wall, but the people living near the Jews wanted to stop the construction. They made plans to destroy all the work Nehemiah and his workers had done. But Nehemiah wouldn't give up; he knew he had to get the wall built, and he knew God wouldn't let him fail. Here's more of what Nehemiah wrote:

So I stationed some people behind the lowest parts of the wall. That's where our enemies could easily attack us. I stationed the people family by family. They had their swords, spears and bows with them.

I looked things over. Then I stood up and spoke to the nobles, the officials and the rest of the people. I said, "Don't be afraid of your enemies. Remember the Lord. He is great and powerful. So fight for your brothers and sisters. Fight for your sons and daughters. Fight for your wives and homes."

Our enemies heard that we knew what they were trying to do. They heard that God had blocked their evil plans. So all of us returned to the wall. Each of us did our own work.

From that day on, half of my men did the work. The other half were given spears, shields, bows and armor. The officers stationed themselves behind all of the people of Judah. The people continued to build the wall. Those who carried supplies did their work with one hand. They held a weapon in the other hand. Each of the builders wore his sword at his side as he worked. But the man who blew the trumpet stayed with me.

Then I spoke to the nobles, the officials and the rest of the people. I said, "This is a big job. It covers a lot of territory. We're separated too far from one another along the wall. When you hear the sound of the trumpet, join us at that location. Our God will fight for us!"

So we continued the work. Half of the men held spears. We worked from the first light of sunrise until the stars came out at night. At that time I also spoke to the people. I told them, "Have every man and his helper stay inside Jerusalem at night. Then they can guard us at night. And they can work during the day."

My relatives and I didn't take our clothes off. My men and the guards didn't take theirs off either. Each man kept his weapon with him, even when he went to get water.

Finally Jerusalem, God's holy city, had a wall to protect it! The wall was finished. It was time to celebrate. The people had their first official worship service in Jerusalem.

All of them gathered together. They went to the open area in front of the Water Gate. They told Ezra to bring out the Scroll of the Law of Moses. The LORD had given Israel that law so they would obey him. Ezra was a teacher of the law.

The priest Ezra brought the Law out to the whole community. It was the first day of the seventh month. The group was made up of men and women and everyone who was old enough to understand what Ezra was going to read.

He read the Law to them from sunrise until noon. He did it as he faced the open area in front of the Water Gate. He read it to the men, women and others who could understand. And all of the people paid careful attention as Ezra was reading the Scroll of the Law.

Ezra opened the scroll. All of the people could see him. That's because he was standing above them. As he opened the scroll, the people stood up. Ezra praised the LORD. He is the great God. All of the people lifted up their hands. They said, "Amen! Amen!" Then they bowed down. They turned their faces toward the ground. And they worshiped the LORD.

Then Nehemiah and Ezra spoke up. So did the Levites who were teaching the people. All of those men said to the people, "This day is set apart to honor the LORD your God. So don't sob. Don't be sad."

Nehemiah said, "Go and enjoy some good food and sweet drinks. Send some of it to those who don't have any. This day is set apart to honor our Lord. So don't be sad. The joy of the LORD makes you strong."

Then all of the people went away to eat and drink. They shared their food with others. They celebrated with great joy.

Many of the Jews in Babylon moved back to Judah and settled there. Different countries battled over Judah from time to time. Four hundred years passed. The Roman empire was the strongest power in the world. The Romans took over the land of Judah and made the Jews obey their rules. During this hard time for the Jews, God was working on his plan. Soon the promise he had made through Isaiah would come true. The Messiah was coming.

Discussion Questions

1. Did you ever work very hard on a project or homework assignment, only to lose it all before you could finish it and have to start all over again? What happened and how did it make you feel?
2. What do you like to do when you celebrate birthdays or holidays? Are these family traditions or personal likes and ideas?
3. Do you ever celebrate what God has given you and does for you? How do you celebrate?

22

The Birth of the King

John wrote about Jesus by calling him "the Word." Whenever you hear or read "the Word," you can replace it with "Jesus." Here's what John wrote:

In the beginning, the Word was already there. The Word was with God, and the Word was God. He was with God in the beginning.

All things were made through him. Nothing that has been made was made without him. Life was in him, and that life was the light for all people. The light shines in the darkness. But the darkness has not understood it.

The true light that gives light to every man was coming into the world.

The Word was in the world that was made through him. But the world did not recognize him. He came to what was his own. But his own people did not accept him.

Some people did accept him. They believed in his name. He gave them the right to become children of God. To be a child of God has nothing to do with human parents. Children of God are not born because of human choice or because a husband wants them to be born. They are born because of what God does.

The Word became a human being. He made his home with us. We have seen his glory. It is the glory of the one and only Son. He came from the Father. And he was full of grace and truth.

Moses gave us the law. Jesus Christ has given us grace and truth. No one has ever seen God. But God, the one and only Son, is at the Father's side. He has shown us what God is like.

Here is the story of Jesus' birth according to Luke:

God sent the angel Gabriel to Nazareth, a town in Galilee. He was sent to a virgin. The girl was engaged to a man named Joseph. He came from the family line of David. The virgin's name was Mary. The angel greeted her and said, "The Lord has given you special favor. He is with you."

Mary was very upset because of his words. She wondered what kind of greeting this could be. But the angel said to her, "Do not be afraid, Mary. God is very pleased with you. You will become pregnant and give birth to a son. You must name him Jesus. He will be great and will be called the Son of the Most High God. The Lord God will make him a king like his father David of long ago. He will rule forever over his people, who came from Jacob's family. His kingdom will never end."

"How can this happen?" Mary asked the angel. "I am a virgin."

The angel answered, "The Holy Spirit will come to you. The power of the Most High God will cover you. So the holy one that is born will be called the Son of God."

"I serve the Lord," Mary answered. "May it happen to me just as you said it would." Then the angel left her.

Mary said,

"My soul gives glory to the Lord.
  My spirit delights in God my Savior.
He has taken note of me
  even though I am not important.
From now on all people will call me blessed.
  The Mighty One has done great things for me.
  His name is holy.
He shows his mercy to those who have respect for him,
  from parent to child down through the years.
He has done mighty things with his arm.
  He has scattered those who are proud in their
      deepest thoughts.
He has brought down rulers from their thrones.
  But he has lifted up people who are not important.
He has filled those who are hungry with good things.
  But he has sent those who are rich away empty.
He has helped the people of Israel, who serve him.
  He has always remembered to be kind
to Abraham and his children down through the years.
  He has done it just as he said to our people of long ago."

Although Joseph and Mary were engaged, they weren't married yet, and neither one had ever tried to have a baby. So when Mary told Joseph she was pregnant, Joseph was surprised. After all, Mary was the first and only woman God made pregnant this special way.

Her husband Joseph was a godly man. He did not want to put her to shame in public. So he planned to divorce her quietly.

But as Joseph was thinking about this, an angel of the Lord appeared to him in a dream. The angel said, "Joseph, son of David, don't be afraid to take Mary home as your wife. The baby inside her is from the Holy Spirit. She is going to have a son. You must give him the name Jesus. That is because he will save his people from their sins."

All of this took place to bring about what the Lord had said would happen. He had said through the prophet, "The virgin is going to have a baby. She will give birth to a son. And he will be called Immanuel." The name Immanuel means "God with us."

Joseph woke up. He did what the angel of the Lord commanded him to do. He took Mary home as his wife.

In those days, Caesar Augustus made a law. It required that a list be made of everyone in the whole Roman world ... All went to their own towns to be listed.

So Joseph went also. He went from the town of Nazareth in Galilee to Judea. That is where Bethlehem, the town of David, was. Joseph went there because he belonged to the family line of David. He went there with Mary to be listed. Mary was engaged to him. She was expecting a baby.

While Joseph and Mary were there, the time came for the child to be born. She gave birth to her first baby. It was a boy. She wrapped him in large strips of cloth. Then she placed him in a manger. There was no room for them in the inn.

There were shepherds living out in the fields nearby. It was night, and they were looking after their sheep. An angel of the Lord appeared to them. And the glory of the Lord shone around them. They were terrified.

But the angel said to them, "Do not be afraid. I bring you good news of great joy. It is for all the people. Today in the town of David a Savior has been born to you. He is Christ the Lord. Here is how you will know I am telling you the truth. You will find a baby wrapped in strips of cloth and lying in a manger."

Suddenly a large group of angels from heaven also appeared. They were praising God. They said,

"May glory be given to God in the highest heaven!
And may peace be given to those he is pleased with
on earth!"

The angels left and went into heaven. Then the shepherds said to one another, "Let's go to Bethlehem. Let's see this thing that has happened, which the Lord has told us about."

So they hurried off and found Mary and Joseph and the baby. The baby was lying in the manger. After the shepherds had seen him, they told everyone. They reported what the angel had said about this child. All who heard it were amazed at what the shepherds said to them.

But Mary kept all these things like a secret treasure in her heart. She thought about them over and over.

The shepherds returned. They gave glory and praise to God. Everything they had seen and heard was just as they had been told.

After Jesus' birth, Wise Men from the east came to Jerusalem. They asked, "Where is the child who has been born to be king of the Jews? When we were in the east, we saw his star. Now we have come to worship him."

When King Herod heard about it, he was very upset. Everyone in Jerusalem was troubled too.

King Herod was afraid Jesus would become king instead of him. So he decided to get rid of Jesus. When God told Joseph what Herod wanted to do, he moved his family to Egypt so Jesus would be safe. When Herod finally died, they moved back home.

Every year Jesus' parents went to Jerusalem for the Passover Feast. When he was 12 years old, they went up to the Feast as usual.

After the Feast was over, his parents left to go back home. The boy Jesus stayed behind in Jerusalem. But they were not aware of it. They thought he was somewhere in their group. So they traveled on for a day.

Then they began to look for him among their relatives and friends. They did not find him. So they went back to Jerusalem to look for him. After three days they found him in the temple courtyard. He was sitting with the teachers. He was listening to them and asking them questions. Everyone who heard him was amazed at how much he understood. They also were amazed at his answers.

When his parents saw him, they were amazed. His mother said to him, "Son, why have you treated us like this? Your father and I have been worried about you. We have been looking for you everywhere."

"Why were you looking for me?" he asked. "Didn't you know I had to be in my Father's house?" But they did not understand what he meant by that.

Then he went back to Nazareth with them, and he obeyed them. But his mother kept all these things like a secret treasure in her heart. Jesus became wiser and stronger. He also became more and more pleasing to God and to people.

Discussion Questions

1. Is there someone in your life who has a baby or young child? Do you know what you were like as a baby or young child? Tell a story about yourself that you have heard someone else tell about you, or talk about a memory you have of yourself as a young child.
2. Have you ever gotten lost? How did it happen and what did you do?
3. How can you become "more pleasing to God and to people" (like Jesus as he grew up)?

23

Jesus' Ministry Begins

The Bible doesn't tell us what Jesus did between the ages of twelve and thirty. Jesus probably learned to be a carpenter like Joseph, and he probably played with his friends. One of his friends might have been his cousin John. John was a very special person to God too. Around the time Mary was visited by the angel, the same angel came to tell John's parents that John would be born soon. And the angel also said John would tell the world that the Messiah—Jesus—had finally come.

In those days John the Baptist came and preached in the Desert of Judea. He said, "Turn away from your sins! The kingdom of heaven is near."

John's clothes were made out of camel's hair. He had a leather belt around his waist. His food was locusts and wild honey. People went out to him from Jerusalem and all of Judea. They also came from the whole area around the Jordan River. When they admitted they had sinned, John baptized them in the Jordan.

Jesus came from Galilee to the Jordan River. He wanted to be baptized by John. But John tried to stop him. He told Jesus, "I need to be baptized by you. So why do you come to me?"

Jesus replied, "Let it be this way for now. It is right for us to do this. It carries out God's holy plan." Then John agreed.

As soon as Jesus was baptized, he came up out of the water. At that moment heaven was opened. Jesus saw the Spirit of God coming down on him like a dove.

A voice from heaven said, "This is my Son, and I love him. I am very pleased with him."

The Holy Spirit led Jesus into the desert. There the devil tempted him. After 40 days and 40 nights of going without eating, Jesus was hungry.

The tempter came to him. He said, "If you are the Son of God, tell these stones to become bread."

Jesus answered, "It is written, 'Man doesn't live only on bread. He also lives on every word that comes from the mouth of God.' "

Then the devil took Jesus to the holy city. He had him stand on the highest point of the temple. "If you are the Son of God," he said, "throw yourself down. It is written,

" 'The Lord will command his angels to take good care of
you.
They will lift you up in their hands.
Then you won't trip over a stone.' "

Jesus answered him, "It is also written, 'Do not put the Lord your God to the test.' "

Finally, the devil took Jesus to a very high mountain. He showed him all the kingdoms of the world and their glory. "If you bow down and worship me," he said, "I will give you all of this."

Jesus said to him, "Get away from me, Satan! It is written, 'Worship the Lord your God. He is the only one you should serve.' "

Then the devil left Jesus. Angels came and took care of him.

After Jesus was tempted in the desert, he started to preach to the people. Meanwhile, John the Baptist kept telling the people to listen to Jesus because he was the

Messiah. But some of the Jewish leaders didn't believe John was telling the truth.

The Jews of Jerusalem sent priests and Levites to ask John who he was. John gave witness to them. He did not try to hide the truth. He spoke to them openly. He said, "I am not the Christ."

They asked him, "Then who are you? Are you Elijah?"

He said, "I am not."

"Are you the Prophet we've been expecting?" they asked.

"No," he answered.

They asked one last time, "Who are you? Give us an answer to take back to those who sent us. What do you say about yourself?"

John replied, using the words of Isaiah the prophet. John said, "I'm the messenger who is calling out in the desert, 'Make the way for the Lord straight.' "

Some Pharisees who had been sent asked him, "If you are not the Christ, why are you baptizing people? Why are you doing that if you aren't Elijah or the Prophet we've been expecting?"

"I baptize people with water," John replied. "But One is standing among you whom you do not know. He is the One who comes after me. I am not good enough to untie his sandals."

This all happened at Bethany on the other side of the Jordan River. That was where John was baptizing.

The next day John saw Jesus coming toward him. John said, "Look! The Lamb of God! He takes away the sin of the world! This is the One I was talking about. I said, 'A man who comes after me is more important than I am. That's because he existed before I was born.' I did not know him. But God wants to make it clear to Israel who this person is. That's the reason I came baptizing with water."

Then John told them, "I saw the Holy Spirit come down from heaven like a dove. The Spirit remained on Jesus. I would not have known him. But the One who sent me to baptize with water told me, 'You will see the Spirit come down and remain on someone. He is the One who will baptize with the Holy Spirit.' I have seen it happen. I give witness that this is the Son of God."

Jesus was ready to start his ministry now and tell the people that he was the Messiah who would save them from all their sins if they would confess and believe. Jesus wanted helpers who would learn from him. These helpers, called disciples, went with Jesus practically everywhere. They saw Jesus do some very amazing things. Simon, one of Jesus' disciples, was worried about his mother-in-law. He told Jesus that she was ill.

So [Jesus] went to her. He took her hand and helped her up. The fever left her. Then she began to serve them.

That evening after sunset, the people brought to Jesus all who were sick. They also brought all who were controlled by demons. All the people in town gathered at the door. Jesus healed many of them. They had all kinds of sicknesses. He also drove out many demons. But he would not let the demons speak, because they knew who he was.

A man who had a skin disease came to Jesus. On his knees he begged Jesus. He said, "If you are willing to make me 'clean,' you can do it."

Jesus was filled with deep concern. He reached out his hand and touched the man. "I am willing to do it," he said. "Be 'clean'!" Right away the disease left him. He was healed.

Jesus sent him away at once. He gave the man a strong warning. "Don't tell this to anyone," he said. "Go and show yourself to the priest. Offer the sacrifices that Moses commanded. It will be a witness to the priest and the people that you are 'clean.'"

But the man went out and started talking right away. He spread the news to everyone. So Jesus could no longer enter a town openly. He stayed outside in lonely places. But people still came to him from everywhere.

A few days later, Jesus entered Capernaum again. The people heard that he had come home. So many people gathered that there was no room left. There was not even room outside the door. And Jesus preached the word to them.

Four of those who came were carrying a man who could not walk. But they could not get him close to Jesus because of the crowd. So they made a hole in the roof above Jesus. Then they lowered the man through it on a mat.

Jesus saw their faith. So he said to the man, "Son, your sins are forgiven."

Some teachers of the law were sitting there. They were thinking, "Why is this fellow talking like that? He's saying a very evil thing! Only God can forgive sins!"

Right away Jesus knew what they were thinking. So he said to them, "Why are you thinking these things? Is it easier to say to this man, 'Your sins are forgiven'? Or to say, 'Get up, take your mat and walk'? I want you to know that the Son of Man has authority on earth to forgive sins."

Then Jesus spoke to the man who could not walk. "I tell you," he said, "get up. Take your mat and go home."

The man got up and took his mat. Then he walked away while everyone watched. All the people were amazed. They praised God and said, "We have never seen anything like this!"

The Pharisees were angry with Jesus because they didn't think he was telling the truth. Jesus was saying he could forgive people's sins, which was something only God could do. The Pharisees didn't think there was any way that Jesus could be the Messiah.

Jesus traveled all over Israel preaching and doing miracles. Before long, huge crowds gathered around him wherever he went.

News about him spread all over Syria. People brought to him all who were ill with different kinds of sicknesses. Some were suffering great pain. Others were controlled by demons. Some were shaking wildly. Others couldn't move at all. And Jesus healed all of them.

Large crowds followed him. Some people came from Galilee, from the area known as the Ten Cities, and from Jerusalem and Judea. Others came from the area across the Jordan River.

Because of the crowd, Jesus told his disciples to get a small boat ready for him. This would keep the people from crowding him. Jesus had healed many people. So those who were sick were pushing forward to touch him.

When people with evil spirits saw him, they fell down in front of him. The spirits shouted, "You are the Son of God!" But Jesus ordered them not to tell who he was.

Jesus didn't want to tell everyone he was the Messiah too quickly, because he first had to teach them what the Messiah had come to do: save the people from sin, not destroy Rome in a battle. Jesus knew that he had to do a lot of teaching to make the people see who the Messiah really was. But first he had to teach his helpers.

Jesus went up on a mountainside. He called for certain people to come to him, and they came. He appointed 12 of them and called them apostles. From that time on they would be with him. He would also send them out to preach. They would have authority to drive out demons.

After this, Jesus traveled around from one town and village to another. He announced the good news of God's kingdom. The Twelve were with him. So were some women who had been healed of evil spirits and sicknesses. One was Mary Magdalene. Seven demons had come out of her. Another was Joanna, the wife of Cuza. He was the manager of Herod's household. Susanna and many others were there also. These women were helping to support Jesus and the Twelve with their own money.

Discussion Questions

1. How can you tell people about Jesus? (Brainstorm some options like blogging, writing in a journal, or working with the children's groups at church.)
2. Do you think you would enjoy eating locusts and honey like John the Baptist? Do you think John

enjoyed it? What are your least favorite foods? What about your favorites?

3. Have you ever been tempted to do something you know God would not like? What did you do about the temptation?
4. After reading this chapter, what do you think of Jesus?

24

No Ordinary Man

The Pharisees were important teachers. They followed all of the rules God had told the Israelites to follow when they were in the desert. The Pharisees even added more rules to follow, and they wanted the people to live the exact same way. But now that the Messiah had come, Jesus' task was to teach some new ideas to the people.

Jesus often used stories—called parables—to teach the people. Parables are stories with a special meaning about the kingdom of heaven. God wanted Jesus to teach the people how to live out the kingdom of heaven on earth.

Jesus said, "What can we say God's kingdom is like? What story can we use to explain it? It is like a mustard seed, which is the smallest seed planted in the ground. But when you plant the seed, it grows. It becomes the largest of all garden plants. Its branches are so big that birds can rest in its shade."

Using many stories like those, Jesus spoke the word to them. He told them as much as they could understand. He did not say anything to them without using a story. But when he was alone with his disciples, he explained everything.

The tax collectors and "sinners" were all gathering around to hear Jesus. But the Pharisees and the teachers of the law were whispering among themselves. They said, "This man welcomes sinners and eats with them."

Then Jesus told them a story. He said, "Suppose one of you has 100 sheep and loses one of them. Won't he leave the 99 in the open country? Won't he go and look for the one lost sheep until he finds it? When he finds it, he will joyfully put it on his shoulders and go home. Then he will call his friends and neighbors together. He will say, 'Be joyful with me. I have found my lost sheep.'

"I tell you, it will be the same in heaven. There will be great joy when one sinner turns away from sin. Yes, there will be more joy than for 99 godly people who do not need to turn away from their sins."

One day an authority on the law stood up to put Jesus to the test. "Teacher," he asked, "what must I do to receive eternal life?"

"What is written in the Law?" Jesus replied. "How do you understand it?"

He answered, " 'Love the Lord your God with all your heart and with all your soul. Love him with all your strength and with all your mind.' And, 'Love your neighbor as you love yourself.' "

"You have answered correctly," Jesus replied. "Do that, and you will live."

But the man wanted to make himself look good. So he asked Jesus, "And who is my neighbor?"

Jesus replied, "A man was going down from Jerusalem to Jericho. Robbers attacked him. They stripped off his clothes and beat him. Then they went away, leaving him almost dead. A priest happened to be going down that same road. When he saw the man, he passed by on the other side. A Levite also came by. When he saw the man, he passed by on the other side too.

But a Samaritan came to the place where the man was. When he saw the man, he felt sorry for him. He went to him, poured olive oil and wine on his wounds and bandaged them. Then he put the man on his own donkey. He took him to an inn and took care of him. The next day he took out two silver coins. He gave them to the owner of the inn. 'Take care of him,' he said. 'When I return, I will pay you back for any extra expense you may have.'

"Which of the three do you think was a neighbor to the man who was attacked by robbers?"

The authority on the law replied, "The one who felt sorry for him."

Jesus told him, "Go and do as he did."

Jesus didn't always tell stories; instead he sometimes preached sermons to the people. He gave this next sermon when a crowd was gathered on a mountainside.

He said,

"Blessed are those who are spiritually needy.
  The kingdom of heaven belongs to them.
Blessed are those who are sad.
  They will be comforted.
Blessed are those who are free of pride.
  They will be given the earth.
Blessed are those who are hungry and thirsty for what is right.
  They will be filled.
Blessed are those who show mercy.
  They will be shown mercy.
Blessed are those whose hearts are pure.
  They will see God.
Blessed are those who make peace.
  They will be called sons of God.
Blessed are those who suffer for doing what is right.
  The kingdom of heaven belongs to them.

"Blessed are you when people make fun of you and hurt you because of me. You are also blessed when they tell all kinds of evil lies about you because of me. Be joyful and glad. Your reward in heaven is great. In the same way, people hurt the prophets who lived long ago.

Jesus also taught the people how to pray by saying:

"When you pray, do not be like those who only pretend to be holy. They love to stand and pray in the synagogues and on the street corners. They want to be seen by others. What I'm about to tell you is true. They have received their complete reward.

"When you pray, go into your room. Close the door and pray to your Father, who can't be seen. He will reward you. Your Father sees what is done secretly.

"When you pray, do not keep talking on and on the way ungodly people do. They think they will be heard because they talk a lot. Do not be like them. Your Father knows what you need even before you ask him.

"This is how you should pray.

"'Our Father in heaven,
may your name be honored.
May your kingdom come.
May what you want to happen be done
  on earth as it is done in heaven.
Give us today our daily bread.
Forgive us our sins,
  just as we also have forgiven those who sin
    against us.
Keep us from falling into sin when we are tempted.
Save us from the evil one.'

"Forgive people when they sin against you. If you do, your Father who is in heaven will also forgive you. But if you do not forgive people their sins, your Father will not forgive your sins."

Jesus told the people not to worry about anything, because God has a plan for everyone and promises to watch over us. Jesus said:

"I tell you, do not worry. Don't worry about your life and what you will eat or drink. And don't worry about your body and what you will wear. Isn't there more to life than eating? Aren't there more important things for the body than clothes?

"Look at the birds of the air. They don't plant or gather crops. They don't put away crops in storerooms. But your Father who is in heaven feeds them. Aren't you worth much more than they are?

"Can you add even one hour to your life by worrying?

"And why do you worry about clothes? See how the wild flowers grow. They don't work or make clothing. But here is what I tell you. Not even Solomon in all of his glory was dressed like one of those flowers.

"If that is how God dresses the wild grass, won't he dress you even better? After all, the grass is here only today. Tomorrow it is thrown into the fire. Your faith is so small!

"So don't worry. Don't say, 'What will we eat?' Or, 'What will we drink?' Or, 'What will we wear?' People who are ungodly run after all of those things. Your Father who is in heaven knows that you need them.

"But put God's kingdom first. Do what he wants you to do. Then all of those things will also be given to you.

"So don't worry about tomorrow. Tomorrow will worry about itself. Each day has enough trouble of its own."

After Jesus taught the people these things, he and his disciples went out on a boat. The disciples were about to get a first-hand lesson about God's power.

When evening came, Jesus said to his disciples, "Let's go over to the other side of the lake." They left the crowd behind. And they took him along in a boat, just as he was. There were also other boats with him.

A wild storm came up. Waves crashed over the boat. It was about to sink. Jesus was in the back, sleeping on a cushion. The disciples woke him up. They said, "Teacher! Don't you care if we drown?"

He got up and ordered the wind to stop. He said to the waves, "Quiet! Be still!" Then the wind died down. And it was completely calm.

He said to his disciples, "Why are you so afraid? Don't you have any faith at all yet?"

They were terrified. They asked each other, "Who is this? Even the wind and the waves obey him!"

Jesus could do more than stop the wind and the waves. Because he was God's Son, Jesus could do miraculous things: he could heal people from deadly diseases and bring people back to life. Jesus also told his disciples to teach others about God and do miracles.

Jesus' miracles helped people believe his teachings were true. Jesus sent the twelve disciples out in groups of two. They preached, told people to confess their sins, and healed many people. Later...

The apostles gathered around Jesus. They told him all they had done and taught. But many people were coming and going. So they did not even have a chance to eat.

Then Jesus said to his apostles, "Come with me by yourselves to a quiet place. You need to get some rest." So they went away by themselves in a boat to a quiet place.

But many people who saw them leaving recognized them. They ran from all the towns and got there ahead of them. When Jesus came ashore, he saw a large crowd. He felt deep concern for them. They were like sheep without a shepherd. So he began teaching them many things.

By that time it was late in the day. His disciples came to him. "There is nothing here," they said. "It's already very late. Send the people away. They can go and buy something to eat in the nearby countryside and villages."

But Jesus answered, "You give them something to eat."

They said to him, "That would take eight months of a person's pay! Should we go and spend that much on bread? Are we supposed to feed them?"

"How many loaves do you have?" Jesus asked. "Go and see."

When they found out, they said, "Five loaves and two fish."

Jesus took the five loaves and the two fish. He looked up to heaven and gave thanks. He broke the loaves into pieces. Then he gave them to his disciples to set in front of the people. He also divided the two fish among them all.

All of them ate and were satisfied. The disciples picked up 12 baskets of broken pieces of bread and fish. The number of men who had eaten was 5,000.

Right away Jesus made the disciples get into the boat. He had them go on ahead of him to the other side of the Sea of Galilee. Then he sent the crowd away. After he had sent them away, he went up on a mountainside by himself to pray. When evening came, he was there alone. The boat was already a long way from land. It was being pounded by the waves because the wind was blowing against it.

Early in the morning, Jesus went out to the disciples. He walked on the lake. They saw him walking on the lake and were terrified. "It's a ghost!" they said. And they cried out in fear.

Right away Jesus called out to them, "Be brave! It is I. Don't be afraid."

"Lord, is it you?" Peter asked. "If it is, tell me to come to you on the water."

"Come," Jesus said.

So Peter got out of the boat. He walked on the water toward Jesus. But when Peter saw the wind, he was afraid. He began to sink. He cried out, "Lord! Save me!"

Right away Jesus reached out his hand and caught him. "Your faith is so small!" he said. "Why did you doubt me?"

When they climbed into the boat, the wind died down. Then those in the boat worshiped Jesus. They said, "You really are the Son of God!"

Some of the people who had eaten the bread and fish Jesus had multiplied found Jesus again. Jesus knew they were looking for him only because he performed miracles, not because they wanted to follow his teachings. Jesus told the people he was better than the miracle bread they had eaten. The miracle bread had filled their stomachs, but he was the bread of life, who would fill them spiritually and give them eternal life.

The people were confused by what Jesus said, because if Jesus was the bread of life, he was saying he came from heaven. They weren't sure they believed in Jesus anymore.

From this time on, many of his disciples turned back. They no longer followed him.

"You don't want to leave also, do you?" Jesus asked the Twelve.

Simon Peter answered him, "Lord, who can we go to? You have the words of eternal life. We believe and know that you are the Holy One of God."

Then Jesus replied, "Didn't I choose you, the 12 disciples? But one of you is a devil!" He meant Judas, the son of Simon Iscariot. Judas was one of the Twelve. But later he was going to hand Jesus over to his enemies.

Jesus was a good teacher, but that wasn't the only reason God put him on earth. For two years Jesus taught the people what God wanted them to do. Now the world was ready for the next part of God's plan—Jesus was going to show the people he was the Messiah they had been waiting for.

Discussion Questions

1. Have you ever helped a friend or sibling when they were hurting? Have you ever listened to them talk about their troubles? How does being the helper and listener make you feel?
2. What does it mean to you to have a "pure heart"?
3. Peter was afraid to get out of the boat and go to Jesus on the water. Have you ever tried something new even though you were afraid? What did you do? How did you get through it?

25

Jesus, the Son of God

Jesus had an important question for his apostles. He asked:

"Who do people say I am?"

They replied, "Some say John the Baptist. Others say Elijah. Still others say one of the prophets."

"But what about you?" he asked. "Who do you say I am?"

Peter answered, "You are the Christ."

Jesus warned them not to tell anyone about him.

Jesus wanted to keep his real identity secret until the right time came. So Jesus kept teaching.

Jesus called the crowd to him along with his disciples. He said, "If anyone wants to come after me, he must say no to himself. He must pick up his cross and follow me.

If he wants to save his life, he will lose it. But if he loses his life for me and for the good news, he will save it.

What good is it if someone gains the whole world but loses his soul? Or what can anyone trade for his soul?

"Suppose you are ashamed of me and my words among these adulterous and sinful people. Then the Son of Man will be ashamed of you when he comes in his Father's glory with the holy angels."

During this time, Jesus spent a lot of time traveling with his disciples and teaching them who he was and what would happen to him.

Jesus did not want anyone to know where they were. That was because he was teaching his disciples.

He said to them, "The Son of Man is going to be handed over to men. They will kill him. After three days he will rise from the dead." But they didn't understand what he meant. And they were afraid to ask him about it.

The disciples were having a hard time understanding Jesus' teachings because they still thought the Messiah would be a brave warrior or a fierce king who would save them from the Romans. They didn't understand that the Messiah would save them from their sins instead. And they didn't understand why Jesus had to die.

The Pharisees also had a hard time with Jesus' teachings—but they wanted to kill him. The Pharisees didn't like Jesus' teachings because they were different from what they taught. Jesus also wouldn't obey their rules, and he told people the Pharisees weren't always doing what God wanted. When it was time for the Feast of Tabernacles (a celebration of God's goodness), Jesus had to sneak into the city so the Pharisees wouldn't catch him.

At the Feast the Jews were watching for him. They were asking, "Where is he?"

Many people in the crowd were whispering about him. Some said, "He is a good man."

Others replied, "No. He fools the people."

But no one would say anything about him openly. They were afraid of the Jews.

Jesus did nothing until halfway through the Feast. Then he went up to the temple courtyard and began to teach. The Jews were amazed. They asked, "How did this man learn so much without studying?"

Then some of the people of Jerusalem began asking questions. They said, "Isn't this the man some people are trying to kill? Here he is! He is speaking openly. They aren't saying a word to him. Have the authorities really decided that he is the Christ? But we know where this man is from. When the Christ comes, no one will know where he is from."

Jesus was still teaching in the temple courtyard. He cried out, "Yes, you know me. And you know where I am from. I am not here on my own. The One who sent me is true. You do not know him. But I know him. I am from him, and he sent me."

When he said this, they tried to arrest him. But no one laid a hand on him. His time had not yet come.

Still, many people in the crowd put their faith in him. They said, "How will it be when the Christ comes? Will he do more miraculous signs than this man?"

Jesus spoke to the people again. He said, "I am the light of the world. Those who follow me will never walk in darkness. They will have the light that leads to life."

The Pharisees argued with him. "Here you are," they said, "appearing as your own witness. But your witness does not count."

Jesus answered, "Even if I give witness about myself, my witness does count. I know where I came from. And I know where I am going. But you have no idea where I come from or where I am going.

"If you obey my teaching," he said, "you are really my disciples. Then you will know the truth. And the truth will set you free."

A few months later, Jesus heard that his friend Lazarus had died. Jesus was very upset by the news, and he went to Lazarus's house.

When Jesus arrived, he found out that Lazarus had already been in the tomb for four days. Bethany was less than two miles from Jerusalem. Many Jews had come to Martha and Mary. They had come to comfort them because their brother was dead.

Once more Jesus felt very sad. He came to the tomb. It was a cave with a stone in front of the entrance.

"Take away the stone," he said.

"But, Lord," said Martha, the sister of the dead man, "by this time there is a bad smell. Lazarus has been in the tomb for four days."

Then Jesus said, "Didn't I tell you that if you believed, you would see God's glory?"

So they took away the stone.

Then Jesus looked up. He said, "Father, I thank you for hearing me. I know that you always hear me. But I said this for the benefit of the people standing here. I said it so they will believe that you sent me."

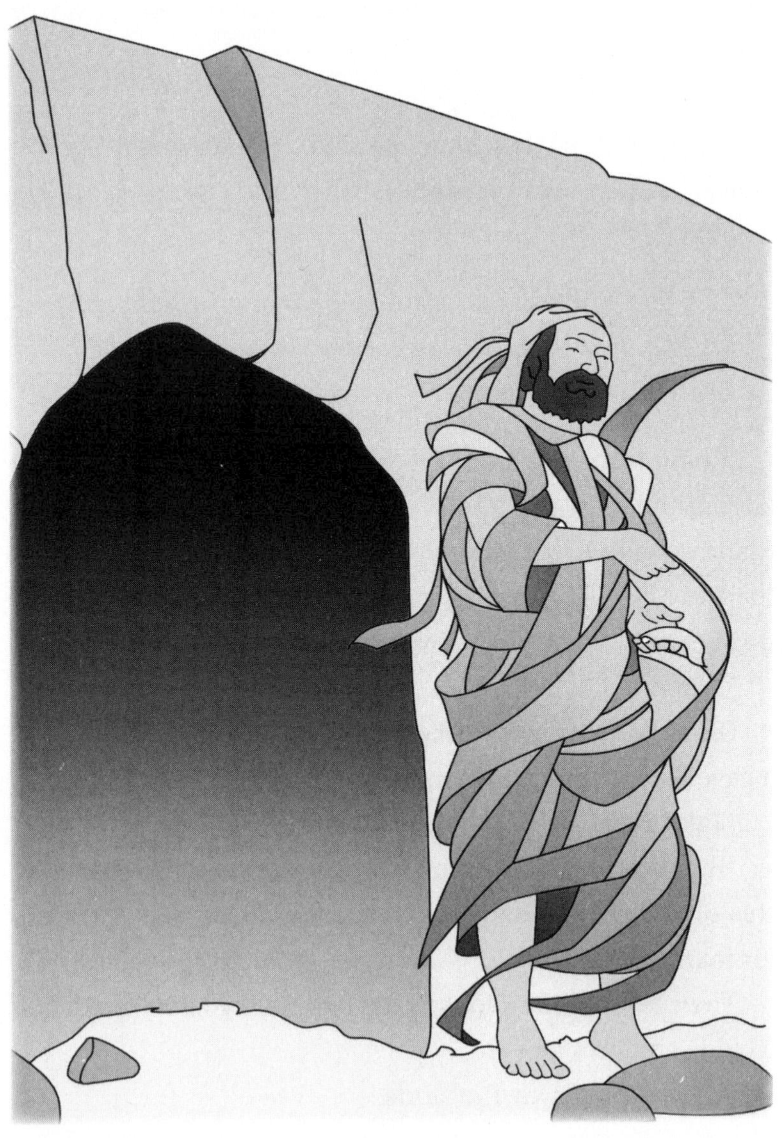

Then Jesus called in a loud voice. He said, "Lazarus, come out!"

The dead man came out. His hands and feet were wrapped with strips of linen. A cloth was around his face.

Jesus said to them, "Take off the clothes he was buried in and let him go."

Many of the Jews who had come to visit Mary saw what Jesus did. So they put their faith in him.

But some of them went to the Pharisees. They told the Pharisees what Jesus had done. Then the chief priests and the Pharisees called a meeting of the Sanhedrin.

"What can we do?" they asked. "This man is doing many miraculous signs. If we let him keep on doing this, everyone will believe in him. Then the Romans will come. They will take away our temple and our nation."

The leaders came up with a plan to get rid of Jesus for good. The Passover Feast was coming soon, and if Jesus came anywhere near Jerusalem to celebrate, they would arrest him. Jesus knew the leaders wanted to kill him, but he started walking toward Jerusalem anyway.

People were bringing little children to Jesus. They wanted him to touch them. But the disciples told the people to stop.

When Jesus saw this, he was angry. He said to his disciples, "Let the little children come to me. Don't keep them away. God's kingdom belongs to people like them. What I'm about to tell you is true. Anyone who will not receive God's kingdom like a little child will never enter it."

Then he took the children in his arms. He put his hands on them and blessed them.

It was almost time for the Jewish Passover Feast. Many people went up from the country to Jerusalem. They went there for the special washing that would make them pure before the Passover Feast. They kept looking for Jesus as they stood in the temple area. They asked one another, "What do you think? Isn't he coming to the Feast at all?"

But the chief priests and the Pharisees had given orders. They had commanded anyone who found out where Jesus was staying to report it. Then they could arrest him.

The time was finally right for everyone to know exactly who the Messiah was. Jesus was going to reveal that he was the Messiah to the people by walking into Jerusalem in a big parade. But first, Jesus had to send two of the disciples into Jerusalem to get something that would show the people he came in peace.

He said to them, "Go to the village ahead of you. Just as you enter it, you will find a donkey's colt tied there. No one has ever ridden it. Untie it and bring it here. Someone may ask you, 'Why are you doing this?' If so, say, 'The Lord needs it. But he will send it back here soon.' "

So they left. They found a colt out in the street. It was tied at a doorway. They untied it. Some people standing there asked, "What are you doing? Why are you untying that colt?" They answered as Jesus had told them to. So the people let them go.

They brought the colt to Jesus. They threw their coats over it. Then he sat on it.

Many people spread their coats on the road. Others spread branches they had cut in the fields. Those in front and those in back shouted,

"Hosanna!"

"Blessed is the one who comes in the name of the Lord!"

"Blessed is the coming kingdom of our father David!"

"Hosanna in the highest heaven!"

When Jesus entered Jerusalem, the whole city was stirred up. The people asked, "Who is this?"

The crowds answered, "This is Jesus. He is the prophet from Nazareth in Galilee."

During Passover week, Jesus taught the people and told them he would have to die soon. Since he was human as well as God, Jesus was concerned with what he would have to face. Jesus said:

"My heart is troubled. What should I say? 'Father, save me from this hour'? No. This is the very reason I came to this hour. Father, bring glory to your name!"

Then a voice came from heaven. It said, "I have brought glory to my name. I will bring glory to it again."

The crowd there heard the voice. Some said it was thunder. Others said an angel had spoken to Jesus.

Jesus said, "This voice was for your benefit, not mine. Now it is time for the world to be judged. Now the prince of this world will be thrown out. But I am going to be lifted up from the earth. When I am, I will bring all people to myself." He said this to show them how he was going to die.

Jesus had done all these miraculous signs in front of them. But they still would not believe in him.

At the same time that Jesus did those miracles, many of the leaders believed in him. But because of the Pharisees, they would not admit they believed. They were afraid they would be thrown out of the synagogue. They loved praise from people more than praise from God.

Then Jesus cried out, "Anyone who believes in me does not believe in me only. He also believes in the One who sent me. When he looks at me, he sees the One who sent me.

"I have come into the world to be a light. No one who believes in me will stay in darkness.

"I don't judge a person who hears my words but does not obey them. I didn't come to judge the world. I came to save it. But there is a judge for anyone who does not accept me and my words. The very words I have spoken will judge him on the last day.

"I did not speak on my own. The Father who sent me commanded me what to say. He also told me how to say it. I know that his command leads to eternal life. So everything I say is just what the Father has told me to say."

The Passover and the Feast of Unleavened Bread were only two days away. The chief priests and the teachers of the law were looking for a clever way to arrest Jesus. They wanted to kill him. "But not during the Feast," they said. "The people may stir up trouble."

The leaders were eager to kill Jesus, but they needed to figure out a good way to arrest him. One of Jesus' disciples, named Judas Iscariot, solved the leaders' problem. Judas decided he didn't want to follow Jesus anymore. So he went to talk to the leaders.

Then Satan entered Judas, who was called Iscariot. Judas was one of the Twelve. He went to the chief priests and the officers of the temple guard. He talked with them about how he could hand Jesus over to them. They were delighted and agreed to give him money.

Judas accepted their offer. He watched for the right time to hand Jesus over to them. He wanted to do it when no crowd was around.

Discussion Questions

1. Some people say, "Hosanna!" when they praise Jesus. What do you say or sing when you praise Jesus?
2. Why do you think people didn't want to believe Jesus was the Savior?
3. Why do you think Jesus went back to Jerusalem, even though he knew some people wanted to kill him? Can you imagine believing in something that much?

26
The Hour of Darkness

It was the first day of the Feast of Unleavened Bread. That was the time to sacrifice the Passover lamb.

Jesus' disciples asked him, "Where do you want us to go and prepare for you to eat the Passover meal?"

So he sent out two of his disciples. He told them, "Go into the city. A man carrying a jar of water will meet you. Follow him. He will enter a house. Say to its owner, 'The Teacher asks, "Where is my guest room? Where can I eat the Passover meal with my disciples?"' He will show you a large upstairs room. It will have furniture and will be ready. Prepare for us to eat there."

The disciples left and went into the city. They found things just as Jesus had told them. So they prepared the Passover meal.

When evening came, Jesus arrived with the Twelve.

While the disciples were eating their Passover meal, Jesus was thinking about what was going to happen to him. Then Jesus said something that really surprised the disciples.

Jesus' spirit was troubled. Here is the witness he gave. "What I'm about to tell you is true," he said. "One of you is going to hand me over to my enemies."

His disciples stared at one another. They had no idea which one of them he meant.

"Lord, who is it?"

Jesus answered, "It is the one I will give this piece of bread to. I will give it to him after I have dipped it in the dish."

He dipped the piece of bread. Then he gave it to Judas Iscariot, son of Simon. As soon as Judas took the bread, Satan entered into him.

"Do quickly what you are going to do," Jesus told him.

But no one at the meal understood why Jesus said this to him. Judas was in charge of the money. So some of the disciples thought Jesus was telling him to buy what was needed for the Feast. Others thought Jesus was talking about giving something to poor people.

As soon as Judas had taken the bread, he went out. And it was night.

After Judas left, Jesus told the disciples what was going to happen. He explained that his body would be broken like the bread, and his blood would be poured out like the wine.

While they were eating, Jesus took bread. He gave thanks and broke it. He handed it to his disciples and said, "Take this and eat it. This is my body."

Then he took the cup. He gave thanks and handed it to them. He said, "All of you drink from it. This is my blood of the new covenant. It is poured out to forgive the sins of many.

"Do not let your hearts be troubled. Trust in God. Trust in me also.

"There are many rooms in my Father's house. If this were not true, I would have told you. I am going there to prepare a place for you. If I go and do that, I will come back. And I will take you to be with me. Then you will also be where I am.

"You know the way to the place where I am going."

Thomas said to him, "Lord, we don't know where you are going. So how can we know the way?"

Jesus answered, "I am the way and the truth and the life. No one comes to the Father except through me. If you really knew me, you would know my Father also. From now on, you do know him. And you have seen him."

Philip said, "Lord, show us the Father. That will be enough for us."

Jesus answered, "Don't you know me, Philip? I have been among you such a long time! Anyone who has seen me has seen the Father. So how can you say, 'Show us the Father'?

"Don't you believe that I am in the Father? Don't you believe that the Father is in me? The words I say to you are not just my own. The Father lives in me. He is the One who is doing his work. Believe me when I say I am in the Father. Also believe that the Father is in me. Or at least believe what the miracles show about me.

"What I'm about to tell you is true. Anyone who has faith in me will do what I have been doing. In fact, he will do even greater things. That is because I am going to the Father.

"And I will do anything you ask in my name. Then the Son will bring glory to the Father. You may ask me for anything in my name. I will do it.

"If you love me, you will obey what I command."

Jesus tried to help his disciples understand what was going to happen to him, but he knew the disciples would still get scared. He said that some of the disciples might run away when the soldiers came, and that they would even tell people they didn't know Jesus so they wouldn't get hurt. But a disciple named Peter was feeling brave.

Peter replied, "All the others may turn away because of you. But I never will."

"What I'm about to tell you is true," Jesus answered. "It will happen this very night. Before the rooster crows, you will say three times that you don't know me."

But Peter said, "I may have to die with you. But I will never say I don't know you." And all the other disciples said the same thing.

Then Jesus went with his disciples to a place called Gethsemane. He said to them, "Sit here while I go over there and pray."

He took Peter and the two sons of Zebedee along with him. He began to be sad and troubled. Then he said to them, "My soul is very sad. I feel close to death. Stay here. Keep watch with me."

He went a little farther. Then he fell with his face to the ground. He prayed, "My Father, if it is possible, take this cup of suffering away from me. But let what you want be done, not what I want."

Then he returned to his disciples and found them sleeping. "Couldn't you men keep watch with me for one hour?" he asked Peter. "Watch and pray. Then you won't fall into sin when you are tempted. The spirit is willing. But the body is weak."

Jesus went away a second time. He prayed, "My Father, is it possible for this cup to be taken away? But if I must drink it, may what you want be done."

An angel from heaven appeared to Jesus and gave him strength. Because he was very sad and troubled, he prayed even harder. His sweat was like drops of blood falling to the ground.

Then he came back. Again he found them sleeping. They couldn't keep their eyes open. So he left them and went away once more. For the third time he prayed the same thing.

Then he returned to the disciples. He said to them, "Are you still sleeping and resting? Look! The hour is near. The Son of Man is about to be handed over to sinners. Get up! Let us go! Here comes the one who is handing me over to them!"

While Jesus was still speaking, Judas arrived. He was one of the Twelve. A large crowd was with him. They were carrying swords and clubs. The chief priests and the elders of the people had sent them.

Jesus knew everything that was going to happen to him. So he went out and asked them, "Who is it that you want?"

"Jesus of Nazareth," they replied.

"I am he," Jesus said.

Judas, who was going to hand Jesus over, was standing there with them. When Jesus said, "I am he," they moved back. Then they fell to the ground.

He asked them again, "Who is it that you want?"

They said, "Jesus of Nazareth."

"I told you I am he," Jesus answered. "If you are looking for me, then let these men go." This happened so that the words Jesus had spoken would come true. He had said, "I have not lost anyone God has given me."

Simon Peter had a sword and pulled it out. He struck the high priest's servant and cut off his right ear.

But Jesus answered, "Stop this!" And he touched the man's ear and healed him.

Jesus knew that these bad things had to happen to make sure everything the prophets had said about the Messiah came true. So he didn't resist being arrested.

After the soldiers arrested Jesus, the disciples ran away, just like Jesus had predicted. The soldiers took Jesus to the leaders, who put him on trial. One disciple, named Peter, secretly followed the soldiers and waited outside so he would know how the trial was going.

They started a fire in the middle of the courtyard. Then they sat down together. Peter sat down with them.

A female servant saw him sitting there in the firelight. She looked closely at him. Then she said, "This man was with Jesus."

But Peter said he had not been with him. "Woman, I don't know him," he said.

A little later someone else saw Peter. "You also are one of them," he said.

"No," Peter replied. "I'm not!"

About an hour later, another person spoke up. "This fellow must have been with Jesus," he said. "He is from Galilee."

Peter replied, "Man, I don't know what you're talking about!"

Just as he was speaking, the rooster crowed. The Lord turned and looked right at Peter. Then Peter remembered what the Lord had spoken to him. "The rooster will crow today," Jesus had said. "Before it does, you will say three times that you don't know me." Peter went outside. He broke down and sobbed.

During the trial, the leaders found a reason to put Jesus to death. Jesus told the leaders he was God's Son, but the leaders thought he was lying. According to the leaders' rules, people who lied about being God had to die. Since the leaders couldn't kill Jesus themselves, they took him to a Roman governor named Pilate. Pilate knew Jesus hadn't done anything wrong, but he still said Jesus had to die.

Then Pilate took Jesus and had him whipped. The soldiers twisted thorns together to make a crown. They put it on Jesus' head. Then they put a purple robe on him. They went up to him again and again. They kept saying, "We honor you, king of the Jews!" And they hit him in the face.

Once more Pilate came out. He said to the Jews, "Look, I am bringing Jesus out to you. I want to let you know that I find no basis for a charge against him."

Jesus came out wearing the crown of thorns and the purple robe. Then Pilate said to them, "Here is the man!"

As soon as the chief priests and their officials saw him, they shouted, "Crucify him! Crucify him!"

But Pilate answered, "You take him and crucify him. I myself find no basis for a charge against him."

The Jews replied, "We have a law. That law says he must die. He claimed to be the Son of God."

Finally, Pilate handed Jesus over to them to be nailed to a cross.

On their way out of the city, they met a man from Cyrene. His name was Simon. They forced him to carry the cross.

Two other men were also led out with Jesus to be killed. Both of them had broken the law. The soldiers brought them to the place called The Skull. There they nailed Jesus to the cross. He hung between the two criminals. One was on his right and one was on his left.

Jesus said, "Father, forgive them. They don't know what they are doing." The soldiers divided up his clothes by casting lots.

The people stood there watching. The rulers even made fun of Jesus. They said, "He saved others. Let him save himself if he is the Christ of God, the Chosen One."

The soldiers also came up and poked fun at him. They offered him wine vinegar. They said, "If you are the king of the Jews, save yourself."

A written sign had been placed above him. It read, THIS IS THE KING OF THE JEWS.

One of the criminals hanging there made fun of Jesus. He said, "Aren't you the Christ? Save yourself! Save us!"

But the other criminal scolded him. "Don't you have any respect for God?" he said. "Remember, you are under the same sentence of death. We are being punished fairly. We are getting just what our actions call for. But this man hasn't done anything wrong."

Then he said, "Jesus, remember me when you come into your kingdom."

Jesus answered him, "What I'm about to tell you is true. Today you will be with me in paradise."

For long, painful hours, Jesus hung on the cross. Not only did his hands and feet hurt where nails had been pounded into him, but breathing was very hard. Jesus had to pull himself up with his tired, painful arms each time he had to breathe, and as time passed he had less and less energy and more and more pain to deal with.

It was now about noon. The whole land was covered with darkness until three o'clock. The sun had stopped shining.

About three o'clock, Jesus cried out in a loud voice. He said, *"Eloi, Eloi, lama sabachthani?"* This means "My God, my God, why have you deserted me?"

Some of those standing there heard Jesus cry out. They said, "He's calling for Elijah."

Right away one of them ran and got a sponge. He filled it with wine vinegar and put it on a stick. He offered it to Jesus to drink. The rest said, "Leave him alone. Let's see if Elijah comes to save him."

After Jesus drank he said, "It is finished." Then he bowed his head and died.

At that moment the temple curtain was torn in two from top to bottom. The earth shook. The rocks split. Tombs broke open. The bodies of many holy people who had died were raised to life. They came out of the tombs. After Jesus was raised to life, they went into the holy city. There they appeared to many people.

The Roman commander and those guarding Jesus saw the earthquake and all that had happened. They were terrified. They exclaimed, "He was surely the Son of God!"

The people had gathered to watch that sight. When they saw what happened, they beat their chests and went away. But all those who knew Jesus stood not very far away, watching those things. They included the women who had followed him from Galilee.

Discussion Questions

1. How is communion celebrated at your church (or at the churches you have visited)?
2. Peter denied knowing Jesus three times. Do you think you would have denied knowing Jesus? Do you tell others that you believe in Jesus?
3. Why did Jesus die for our sins?

27

The Resurrection

Jesus was dead, and his followers were incredibly sad. They forgot Jesus said he wouldn't stay dead forever. Once Jesus' body was taken down off the cross, two of Jesus' friends buried it in a cave tomb. Then they rolled a large, heavy stone in front of the opening to close it.

But the Jewish leaders remembered that Jesus promised to come back to life in three days. They put soldiers in front of the tomb to make sure no one tried to steal Jesus' body to pretend he was alive. No one really thought Jesus would come back to life. But on the morning of the third day, something surprising happened.

There was a powerful earthquake. An angel of the Lord came down from heaven. The angel went to the tomb. He rolled back the stone and sat on it. His body shone like lightning. His clothes were as white as snow. The guards were so afraid of him that they shook and became like dead men.

The angel said to the women, "Don't be afraid. I know that you are looking for Jesus, who was crucified. He is not here! He has risen, just as he said he would! Come and see the place where he was lying. Go quickly! Tell his disciples, 'He has risen from the dead. He is going ahead of you into Galilee. There you will see him.' Now I have told you."

So the women hurried away from the tomb. They were afraid, but they were filled with joy. They ran to tell the disciples.

So Peter and the other disciple started out for the tomb. Both of them were running. The other disciple ran faster than Peter. He reached the tomb first. He bent over and looked in at the strips of linen lying there. But he did not go in.

Then Simon Peter, who was behind him, arrived. He went into the tomb. He saw the strips of linen lying there. He also saw the burial cloth that had been around Jesus' head. The cloth was folded up by itself. It was separate from the linen.

The disciple who had reached the tomb first also went inside. He saw and believed. They still did not understand from Scripture that Jesus had to rise from the dead.

Then the disciples went back to their homes.

The disciples were still talking about this when Jesus himself suddenly stood among them. He said, "May peace be with you!"

They were surprised and terrified. They thought they were seeing a ghost.

Jesus said to them, "Why are you troubled? Why do you have doubts in your minds? Look at my hands and my feet. It is really I! Touch me and see. A ghost does not have a body or bones. But you can see that I do."

After he said that, he showed them his hands and feet. But they still did not believe it. They were amazed and filled with joy.

So Jesus asked them, "Do you have anything here to eat?"

They gave him a piece of cooked fish. He took it and ate it in front of them.

Jesus said to them, "This is what I told you while I was still with you. Everything written about me must happen. Everything written about me in the Law of Moses, the Prophets and the Psalms must come true."

Then he opened their minds so they could understand the Scriptures. He told them, "This is what is written. The

Christ will suffer. He will rise from the dead on the third day. His followers will preach in his name. They will tell others to turn away from their sins and be forgiven. People from every nation will hear it, beginning at Jerusalem. You have seen these things with your own eyes.

"I am going to send you what my Father has promised. But for now, stay in the city. Stay there until you have received power from heaven."

After this, Jesus appeared to his disciples again. It was by the Sea of Galilee. Here is what happened.

Simon Peter and Thomas, who was called Didymus, were there together. Nathanael from Cana in Galilee and the sons of Zebedee were with them. So were two other disciples.

"I'm going out to fish," Simon Peter told them. They said, "We'll go with you." So they went out and got into the boat. That night they didn't catch anything.

Early in the morning, Jesus stood on the shore. But the disciples did not realize that it was Jesus.

He called out to them, "Friends, don't you have any fish?"

"No," they answered.

He said, "Throw your net on the right side of the boat. There you will find some fish."

When they did, they could not pull the net into the boat. There were too many fish in it.

It took a while for the disciples to really understand Jesus was back, and what his resurrection meant. Jesus reminded them of his teachings so things would make sense to them. The disciples needed to know why Jesus died and came back to life because they would need to tell everyone else what they had seen and heard.

Then the 11 disciples went to Galilee. They went to the mountain where Jesus had told them to go. When they saw him, they worshiped him. But some still had their doubts.

Then Jesus came to them. He said, "All authority in heaven and on earth has been given to me. So you must go and make disciples of all nations. Baptize them in the name of the Father and of the Son and of the Holy Spirit. Teach them to obey everything I have commanded you. And you can be sure that I am always with you, to the very end."

Discussion Questions

1. Why do you think Jesus was resurrected from the dead?
2. How do you think Jesus knew there were all those fish on the other side of the boat? Do you believe in miracles? Have you ever experienced a miracle or heard about someone else experiencing a miracle?
3. How can you tell or show others about what Jesus taught the disciples?

28

New Beginnings

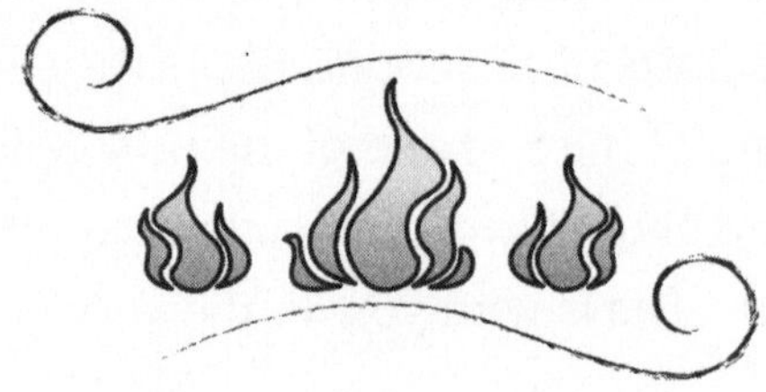

Before Jesus left, he gave orders to the apostles he had chosen. He did this through the Holy Spirit. After his suffering and death, he appeared to them. In many ways he proved that he was alive. He appeared to them over a period of 40 days. During that time he spoke about God's kingdom.

One day Jesus was eating with them. He gave them a command. "Do not leave Jerusalem," he said. "Wait for the gift my Father promised. You have heard me talk about it. John baptized with water. But in a few days you will be baptized with the Holy Spirit."

When the apostles met together, they asked Jesus a question. "Lord," they said, "are you going to give the kingdom back to Israel now?"

He said to them, "You should not be concerned about times or dates. The Father has set them by his own authority. But you will receive power when the Holy Spirit comes on you. Then you will be my witnesses in Jerusalem. You will be my witnesses in all Judea and Samaria. And you will be my witnesses from one end of the earth to the other."

After Jesus said this, he was taken up to heaven. They watched until a cloud hid him from their sight.

While he was going up, they kept on looking at the sky. Suddenly two men dressed in white clothing stood beside them. "Men of Galilee," they said, "why do you stand here looking at the sky? Jesus has been taken away from you into heaven. But he will come back in the same way you saw him go."

The day of Pentecost came. The believers all gathered in one place. Suddenly a sound came from heaven. It was like a strong wind blowing. It filled the whole house where they were sitting. They saw something that looked like tongues of fire. The flames separated and settled on each of them. All of them were filled with the Holy Spirit. They began to speak in languages they had not known before. The Spirit gave them the ability to do this.

Godly Jews from every country in the world were staying in Jerusalem. A crowd came together when they heard the sound. They were bewildered because they each heard the believers speaking in their own language.

The Holy Spirit came to help the disciples tell people about Jesus and help others believe in Jesus too. But some of the people thought the disciples were just acting crazy. So Peter started telling the crowd all the facts about Jesus.

"Long ago God planned that Jesus would be handed over to you. With the help of evil people, you put Jesus to death. You nailed him to the cross. But God raised him from the dead. He set him free from the suffering of death. It wasn't possible for death to keep its hold on Jesus.

"God has raised this same Jesus back to life. We are all witnesses of this. Jesus has been given a place of honor at the right hand of God. He has received the Holy Spirit from the Father. This is what God had promised. It is Jesus who has poured out what you now see and hear."

Many people became believers of Jesus because of what the apostles taught them.

The believers studied what the apostles taught. They shared life together. They broke bread and ate together. And they prayed. Everyone felt that God was near. The apostles did many wonders and miraculous signs. All the believers were together. They shared everything they had. They sold what they owned. They gave each other everything they needed. Every day they met together in the temple courtyard. In their homes they broke bread and ate together. Their hearts were glad and honest and true. They praised God. They were respected by all the people. Every day the Lord added to their group those who were being saved.

The leaders who hated Jesus didn't like Jesus' followers either. A man named Saul and other Jewish leaders tried to stop the church of believers from adding new people by scaring or even killing them. Many Christians went to other cities so they would be safe, and there they told others about Jesus.

The believers who had been scattered preached the word everywhere they went. Philip went down to a city in Samaria. There he preached about the Christ. The crowds listened to Philip. They saw the miraculous signs he did. They all paid close attention to what he said. Evil spirits screamed and came out of many people. Many who were disabled or who couldn't walk were healed. So there was great joy in that city.

Meanwhile, Saul continued to oppose the Lord's followers. He said they would be put to death. He went to the high priest. He asked the priest for letters to the synagogues in Damascus. He wanted to find men and women who belonged to the Way of Jesus. The letters would allow him to take them as prisoners to Jerusalem.

On his journey, Saul approached Damascus. Suddenly a light from heaven flashed around him. He fell to the ground. He heard a voice speak to him. "Saul! Saul!" the voice said. "Why are you opposing me?"

"Who are you, Lord?" Saul asked.

"I am Jesus," he replied. "I am the one you are opposing. Now get up and go into the city. There you will be told what you must do."

The men traveling with Saul stood there. They weren't able to speak. They had heard the sound. But they didn't see anyone. Saul got up from the ground. He opened his eyes, but he couldn't see. So they led him by the hand into Damascus. For three days he was blind. He didn't eat or drink anything.

In Damascus there was a believer named Ananias. The Lord called out to him in a vision. "Ananias!" he said.

"Yes, Lord," he answered.

The Lord told him, "Go to the house of Judas on Straight Street. Ask for a man from Tarsus named Saul. He is praying. In a vision he has seen a man named Ananias. The man has come and placed his hands on him. Now he will be able to see again."

"Lord," Ananias answered, "I've heard many reports about this man. They say he has done great harm to God's people in Jerusalem. Now he has come here to arrest all those who worship you. The chief priests have given him authority to do this."

But the Lord said to Ananias, "Go! I have chosen this man to work for me. He will carry my name to those who aren't Jews and to their kings. He will bring my name to the people of Israel. I will show him how much he must suffer for me."

Then Ananias went to the house and entered it. He placed his hands on Saul. "Brother Saul," he said, "you saw the Lord Jesus. He appeared to you on the road as you were coming here. He has sent me so that you will be able to see again. You will be filled with the Holy Spirit."

Right away something like scales fell from Saul's eyes. And he could see again. He got up and was baptized. After eating some food, he got his strength back.

Saul's heart had completely changed. Saul started telling people about Jesus, and he changed his name to Paul to show he was a different person. After a while he went to Jerusalem to talk to the disciples (who were now called the apostles) about how he could help the church. The apostles realized Paul really did love Jesus, and that he was a very good preacher. At the direction of the Holy Spirit, they decided to send Paul to other countries to tell the non-Jewish people about Jesus—just like God said would happen.

About this time, King Herod arrested some people who belonged to the church. He planned to make them suffer greatly. He had James killed with a sword. James was John's brother. Herod saw that the death of James pleased the Jews. So he arrested Peter also. This happened during the Feast of Unleavened Bread. After Herod arrested Peter, he put him in prison. Peter was placed under guard. He was watched by four groups of four soldiers each. Herod planned to put Peter on public trial. It would take place after the Passover Feast.

So Peter was kept in prison. But the church prayed hard to God for him.

It was the night before Herod was going to bring him to trial. Peter was sleeping between two soldiers. Two chains held him there. Lookouts stood guard at the entrance. Suddenly an angel of the Lord appeared. A light shone in the prison cell. The angel struck Peter on his side. Peter woke up. "Quick!" the angel said. "Get up!" The chains fell off Peter's wrists.

Then the angel said to him, "Put on your clothes and sandals." Peter did so. "Put on your coat," the angel told him. "Follow me." Peter followed him out of the prison. But he had no idea that what the angel was doing was really happening. He thought he was seeing a vision. They passed the first and second guards. Then they came to the iron gate leading to the city. It opened for them by itself. They went through it. They walked the length of one street. Suddenly the angel left Peter.

Then Peter realized what had happened. He said, "Now I know for sure that the Lord sent his angel. He set me free from Herod's power. He saved me from everything the Jewish people were hoping for."

When Peter understood what had happened, he went to Mary's house. Mary was the mother of John Mark. Many people had gathered in her home. They were praying there. Peter knocked at the outer entrance. A servant named Rhoda came to answer the door. She recognized Peter's voice. She was so excited that she ran back without opening the door. "Peter is at the door!" she exclaimed.

"You're out of your mind," they said to her. But she kept telling them it was true. So they said, "It must be his angel."

Peter kept on knocking. When they opened the door and saw him, they were amazed. Peter motioned with his hand for them to be quiet. He explained how the Lord had brought him out of prison. "Tell James and the others about this," he said. Then he went to another place.

In the morning the soldiers were bewildered. They couldn't figure out what had happened to Peter.

No matter who hurt the new Christians, the Holy Spirit continued to work in the new believers, encouraging them to spread the Good News. Saul (Paul) and his co-workers boldly spoke about Jesus everywhere they went.

Discussion Questions

1. What do you think angels look like? Where did you get your ideas?
2. What does the Holy Spirit mean to you?
3. How can you show others that you are a Christian?

29

Paul's Mission

One of the first people Paul met when he came back to Jerusalem was a man named Barnabas. Barnabas was a very strong believer, and he and Paul became good friends. The Holy Spirit sent Paul and Barnabas to a lot of places to tell people about Jesus and help start churches.

Paul and Barnabas soon had more helpers — two were named Silas and John Mark. John Mark had traveled with them before, but he had gone home early during one of the trips. Barnabas thought John Mark was still a good helper, but Paul disagreed. Paul and Barnabas argued about this and decided to travel separately. Silas went with Paul, and John Mark went with Barnabas.

While Paul traveled with Silas, they met a man named Timothy who also joined them for awhile. Paul, Silas, and Timothy went to many different cities and talked to the people in each place.

One day we were going to the place of prayer. On the way we were met by a female slave. She had a spirit that helped her to tell ahead of time what was going to happen. She earned a lot of money for her owners by telling fortunes. The woman followed Paul and the rest of us around. She shouted, "These men serve the Most High God. They are telling you how to be saved." She kept this up for many days. Finally Paul became upset. Turning around, he spoke to the spirit. "In the name of Jesus Christ," he said, "I command you to come out of her!" At that very moment the spirit left her.

The female slave's owners realized that their hope of making money was gone. So they grabbed Paul and Silas. They dragged them into the market place to face the authorities. They brought them to the judges. "These men are Jews," her owners said. "They are making trouble in our city. They are suggesting practices that are against Roman law. These are practices we can't accept or take part in."

The crowd joined the attack against Paul and Silas. The judges ordered that Paul and Silas be stripped and beaten. They were whipped without mercy. Then they were thrown into prison. The jailer was commanded to guard them carefully. When he received his orders, he put Paul and Silas deep inside the prison. He fastened their feet so they couldn't get away.

About midnight Paul and Silas were praying. They were also singing hymns to God. The other prisoners were listening to them. Suddenly there was a powerful earthquake. It shook the prison from top to bottom. All at once the prison doors flew open. Everybody's chains came loose.

The jailer woke up. He saw that the prison doors were open. He pulled out his sword and was going to kill himself.

He thought the prisoners had escaped. "Don't harm yourself!" Paul shouted. "We are all here!"

The jailer called out for some lights. He rushed in, shaking with fear. He fell down in front of Paul and Silas. Then he brought them out. He asked, "Sirs, what must I do to be saved?"

They replied, "Believe in the Lord Jesus. Then you and your family will be saved." They spoke the word of the Lord to him. They also spoke to all the others in his house.

At that hour of the night, the jailer took Paul and Silas and washed their wounds. Right away he and his whole family were baptized. The jailer brought them into his house. He set a meal in front of them. He and his whole family were filled with joy. They had become believers in God.

Early in the morning the judges sent their officers to the jailer. They ordered him, "Let those men go." The jailer told Paul, "The judges have ordered me to set you and Silas free. You can leave now. Go in peace."

Paul and his helpers traveled to many places where they taught people about Jesus and started churches. Paul's teachings helped the new Christians understand the things Jesus wanted them to do. But after Paul left a city, the people missed his encouragement and teaching. So Paul would send letters to each church filled with advice to help them stay strong Christians.

Paul's letters weren't just for the people who lived a long time ago—they encourage and teach us today too. Here is some of what he wrote to one of the churches:

We always thank God for all of you. We pray for you. We never forget you when we pray to our God and Father. Your work is produced by your faith. Your service is the result of your love. Your strength to continue comes from your hope in our Lord Jesus Christ.

Brothers and sisters, you are loved by God. We know that he has chosen you. Our good news didn't come to you only in words. It came with power. It came with the Holy Spirit's help. He gave us complete faith in what we were preaching. You know how we lived among you for your good.

How can we thank God enough for you because of all the joy that comes only from our God? Night and day we pray very hard that we will see you again. We want to give you what is missing in your faith.

Now may our God and Father himself and our Lord Jesus open up a way for us to come to you. May the Lord make your love grow. May it be like a rising flood. May your love for one another increase. May it also increase for everyone else. May it be just like our love for you. May the Lord give you strength in your hearts. Then you will be holy and without blame in the sight of our God and Father. May that be true when our Lord Jesus comes with all his holy ones.

The Lord himself will come down from heaven. We will hear a loud command. We will hear the voice of the leader of the angels. We will hear a blast from God's trumpet. Many who believe in Christ will have died already. They will rise first. After that, we who are still alive and are left will be caught up together with them. We will be taken up in the clouds. We will meet the Lord in the air. And we will be with him forever.

So cheer each other up with these words of comfort.

Always be joyful. Never stop praying. Give thanks no matter what happens. God wants you to thank him because you believe in Christ Jesus.

Don't put out the Holy Spirit's fire. Don't treat prophecies as if they amount to nothing. Put everything to the test. Hold on to what is good. Stay away from every kind of evil.

God is the God who gives peace. May he make you holy through and through. May your whole spirit, soul and body be kept free from blame. May you be without blame from now until our Lord Jesus Christ comes. The One who has chosen you is faithful. He will do all these things.

Brothers and sisters, pray for us. Greet all the believers with a holy kiss. While the Lord is watching, here is what I command you. Have this letter read to all the believers.

May the grace of our Lord Jesus Christ be with you.

Sometimes the churches forgot the things Paul had told them. At the church in Corinth, people were disobeying Paul's teachings and fighting with each other. Paul sent a letter to help them get along and do the right things. He wrote this:

Brothers and sisters, I ask all of you to agree with one another. I make my appeal in the name of our Lord Jesus Christ. Then you won't take sides. You will be in complete agreement in all that you think.

There is one body. But it has many parts. Even though it has many parts, they make up one body. It is the same with Christ. We were all baptized by one Holy Spirit into one body. It didn't matter whether we were Jews or Greeks, slaves or free people. We were all given the same Spirit to drink.

The body is not made up of just one part. It has many parts. Suppose the foot says, "I am not a hand. So I don't belong to the body." It is still part of the body. And suppose the ear says, "I am not an eye. So I don't belong to the body." It is still part of the body.

If the whole body were an eye, how could it hear? If the whole body were an ear, how could it smell? God has placed each part in the body just as he wanted it to be.

You are the body of Christ. Each one of you is a part of it.

Suppose I speak in the languages of human beings and of angels. If I don't have love, I am only a loud gong or a noisy cymbal. Suppose I have the gift of prophecy. Suppose I can understand all the secret things of God and know everything about him. And suppose I have enough faith to move mountains. If I don't have love, I am nothing at all. Suppose I give everything I have to poor people. And suppose I give my body to be burned. If I don't have love, I get nothing at all.

Love is patient. Love is kind. It does not want what belongs to others. It does not brag. It is not proud. It is not rude. It does not look out for its own interests. It does not easily become angry. It does not keep track of other people's wrongs.

Love is not happy with evil. But it is full of joy when the truth is spoken. It always protects. It always trusts. It always hopes. It never gives up.

Love never fails.

Paul wanted the people to understand that God loved them so much that he sent Jesus to die for their sins. God's love is the greatest kind of love there is. And if we believe in his Son, Jesus, and with the help of the Holy Spirit treat people with love too, we will get to be with God forever.

Death came because of what a man did. Rising from the dead also comes because of what a man did. Because of Adam, all people die. So because of Christ, all will be made alive.

May the grace of the Lord Jesus be with you.

I give my love to all of you who belong to Christ Jesus. Amen.

Because of Jesus, people who believe in him can enjoy freedom. God gives us freedom to decide things for ourselves—he doesn't force us to do anything. But that freedom doesn't mean we can do whatever we want and get away with it. People who believe in Jesus are given the Holy Spirit who helps you want to do what is right.

But the fruit the Holy Spirit produces is love, joy and peace. It is being patient, kind and good. It is being faithful and gentle and having control of oneself. There is no law against things of that kind.

Those who belong to Christ Jesus have nailed their sinful nature to his cross. They don't want what their sinful nature loves and longs for.

Since we live by the Spirit, let us march in step with the Spirit. Let us not become proud. Let us not make each other angry. Let us not want what belongs to others.

Brothers and sisters, may the grace of our Lord Jesus Christ be with your spirit. Amen.

Discussion Questions

1. In some places of the world, believing in Jesus can still be dangerous. Would you tell people you believed in Jesus, even if it meant getting hurt? Why or why not?
2. Have you ever thought about traveling around the world telling others about Jesus? Where would you like to go? If you know someone who has gone on a mission trip, what was their experience?
3. Paul had some advice about how to cheer people up. What is one thing you can do that he recommended?

30

Paul's Final Days

Paul had been traveling and teaching for many years. Paul taught people to share the good news with others, and new churches were established wherever Paul preached. Many leaders and people in the Roman government wanted to stop the churches from growing because they thought Jesus had been a bad person. They also wanted to stop Paul from preaching.

Paul knew he might get caught, but he trusted God. When God told Paul to go to Jerusalem (where things were very dangerous for Christians), Paul decided to go. He stopped at a few cities on the way to say goodbye to his friends as he sailed toward Jerusalem. Here is what he said:

"Now I am going to Jerusalem. The Holy Spirit compels me. I don't know what will happen to me there. I only know that in every city the Spirit warns me. He tells me that I will face prison and suffering. But my life means nothing to me. I only want to finish the race. I want to complete the work the Lord Jesus has given me. He wants me to give witness to others about the good news of God's grace.

"I have spent time with you preaching about the kingdom. I know that none of you will ever see me again. So I tell you today that I am not guilty if anyone has not believed. I haven't let anyone keep me from telling you everything God wants you to do.

"Keep watch over yourselves. Keep watch over all the believers. The Holy Spirit has made you leaders over them. Be shepherds of God's church. He bought it with his own blood."

When Paul had said this, he got down on his knees with all of them and prayed. They all cried as they hugged and kissed him. What hurt them the most was that he had said they would never see his face again. Then they went with him to the ship.

In one of the cities where Paul stopped, a man prophesied that some Jewish leaders would catch Paul. But Paul believed God had a reason for sending him to Jerusalem, so he got back on the boat and continued his journey. When he reached Jerusalem, some Roman soldiers took him for questioning at a nearby military fort. Paul told the soldiers and all the people about what Jesus had done for him on the road to Damascus and how sorry he was for hurting people back then. He then told the crowd that Jesus died to save them from their sin.

The crowd listened to Paul until he said this. Then they shouted, "Kill him! He isn't fit to live!"

They shouted and threw off their coats. They threw dust into the air. So the commanding officer ordered Paul to be taken into the fort. He gave orders for Paul to be whipped and questioned. He wanted to find out why the people were shouting at him like this.

A commander was standing there as they stretched Paul out to be whipped. Paul said to him, "Does the law allow you to whip a Roman citizen who hasn't even been found guilty?"

When the commander heard this, he went to the commanding officer and reported it. "What are you going to do?" the commander asked. "This man is a Roman citizen."

So the commanding officer went to Paul. "Tell me," he asked. "Are you a Roman citizen?"

"Yes, I am," Paul answered.

Then the officer said, "I had to pay a lot of money to become a citizen."

"But I was born a citizen," Paul replied.

Right away those who were about to question him left. Even the officer was alarmed. He realized that he had put Paul, a Roman citizen, in chains.

Since Paul was a Roman, he had special rights that protected him from being killed right away. He would be able to tell his story to a variety of leaders. This was part of God's plan to have Paul witness to as many Roman leaders as possible while he was in prison.

Paul was first sent to talk to the leaders who had hated Jesus. Then he was sent to a Roman governor named Felix.

After talking with Felix, Paul told his story to a new governor named Festus. Just like Felix had done, Festus held a trial to find out if Paul was guilty of anything. Festus knew Paul was innocent too, but he didn't want to make the leaders mad, so he was going to let Paul die. But God made sure Paul arranged a trial with Caesar, the ruler of the Roman empire.

Before Paul left for Rome, he had a trial before a king named Agrippa. Paul told Agrippa and Festus all about his life and how Jesus had saved him, hoping they would believe in Jesus. Then he got on a boat for Rome.

It was decided that [they] would sail for Italy. Paul and some other prisoners were handed over to a Roman commander named Julius. He belonged to the Imperial Guard.

A lot of time had passed. Sailing had already become dangerous. By now it was after the Day of Atonement, a day of fasting. So Paul gave them a warning. "Men," he said, "I can see that our trip is going to be dangerous. The ship and everything in it will be lost. Our own lives will be in danger also."

But the commander didn't listen to what Paul said. Instead, he followed the advice of the pilot and the ship's owner. The harbor wasn't a good place for ships to stay during winter. So most of the people decided we should sail on. They hoped we would reach Phoenix. They wanted to spend the winter there. Phoenix was a harbor in Crete. It faced both southwest and northwest.

A gentle south wind began to blow. They thought that this was what they had been waiting for. So they pulled up the anchor and sailed along the shore of Crete. Before very long, a wind blew down from the island. It had the force of a hurricane. It was called a "northeaster."

The ship was caught by the storm. We could not keep it sailing into the wind. So we gave up and were driven along. We passed the calmer side of a small island called Cauda. We almost lost the lifeboat. So the men lifted it on board. Then they tied ropes under the ship itself to hold it together. They were afraid it would get stuck on the sandbars of Syrtis. They lowered the sea anchor and let the ship be driven along.

We took a very bad beating from the storm. The next day the crew began to throw the ship's contents overboard. On the third day, they even threw the ship's gear overboard with their own hands. The sun and stars didn't appear for many days. The storm was terrible. So we gave up all hope of being saved.

The men had not eaten for a long time. Paul stood up in front of them. "Men," he said, "you should have taken my advice not to sail from Crete. Then you would have avoided this harm and loss.

"Now I beg you to be brave. Not one of you will die. Only the ship will be destroyed. I belong to God and serve him. Last night his angel stood beside me. The angel said, 'Do not be afraid, Paul. You must go on trial in front of Caesar. God has shown his grace by sparing the lives of all those sailing with you.'

"Men, continue to be brave. I have faith in God. It will happen just as he told me. But we must run the ship onto the beach of some island."

On the 14th night we were still being driven across the Sea of Adria. About midnight the sailors had a feeling that they were approaching land. They measured how deep the water was. They found that it was 120 feet deep. A short time later they measured the water again. This time it was 90 feet deep. They were afraid we would crash against the rocks. So they dropped four anchors from the back of the ship. They prayed that daylight would come.

The sailors wanted to escape from the ship. So they let the lifeboat down into the sea. They pretended they were going to lower some anchors from the front of the ship. But Paul spoke to the commander and the soldiers. "These men must stay with the ship," he said. "If they don't, you can't be saved." So the soldiers cut the ropes that held the lifeboat. They let it drift away.

Just before dawn Paul tried to get them all to eat. "For the last 14 days," he said, "you have wondered what would happen. You have gone without food. You haven't eaten anything. Now I am asking you to eat some food. You need it to live. Not one of you will lose a single hair from your head."

After Paul said this, he took some bread and gave thanks to God. He did this where they all could see him. Then he broke it and began to eat. All of them were filled with hope. So they ate some food. There were 276 of us on board. They ate as much as they wanted. They needed to make the ship lighter. So they threw the rest of the grain into the sea.

When daylight came, they saw a bay with a sandy beach. They didn't recognize the place. But they decided to run the ship onto the beach if they could. So they cut the anchors loose and left them in the sea. At the same time, they untied the ropes that held the rudders. They lifted the sail at the front of the ship to the wind. Then they headed for the beach.

But the ship hit a sandbar. So the front of it got stuck and wouldn't move. The back of the ship was broken to pieces by the pounding of the waves.

When the boat was destroyed, all the prisoners were free from their chains, and the soldiers were afraid the prisoners would try to escape. But the commander of the boat knew Paul wouldn't try to swim away, so he made sure Paul and all the prisoners made it to land safely.

When we were safe on shore, we found out that the island was called Malta. The people of the island were unusually kind. It was raining and cold. So they built a fire and welcomed all of us.

Paul gathered some sticks and put them on the fire. A poisonous snake was driven out by the heat. It fastened itself on Paul's hand. The people of the island saw the snake hanging from his hand. They said to each other, "This man must be a

murderer. He escaped from the sea. But Justice won't let him live." Justice was the name of a goddess.

Paul shook the snake off into the fire. He was not harmed. The people expected him to swell up. They thought he would suddenly fall dead. They waited for a long time. But they didn't see anything unusual happen to him. So they changed their minds. They said he was a god.

Publius owned property nearby. He was the chief official on the island. He welcomed us to his home. For three days he took care of us. He treated us with kindness. His father was sick in bed. The man suffered from fever and dysentery. So Paul went in to see him. Paul prayed for him. He placed his hands on him and healed him.

Then the rest of the sick people on the island came. They too were healed. The people of the island honored us in many ways. When we were ready to sail, they gave us the supplies we needed.

After three months on Malta, everyone was rescued by another ship, and Paul was sailing toward Rome again. Once Paul arrived in Rome, he was allowed to live in a house, but a soldier always guarded him to make sure he didn't try to escape. Paul lived in that house for two years. While he was in Rome he preached to people and told them about Jesus. He also wrote letters to the churches and people he had visited during his travels. Then Paul was put to death.

Many other disciples were tortured and killed for believing in Jesus, but just like Paul they never stopped telling people about Jesus. No matter what governments or leaders did, the church continued to grow and grow.

Discussion Questions

1. Describe the last time you saw someone being brave. When was the last time you were brave?
2. Would you like to be stranded on a deserted island? What would you do if you were stranded?

31

Revelation

A man named John was one of Jesus' disciples, and he was also one of Jesus' best friends. After Jesus died, John became one of the leaders of the Christians.

When John was an old man, he was captured and sent to an island called Patmos for the rest of his life. While he was there, he started seeing visions of heaven and what things would be like when Jesus came back to earth. He wrote down everything he saw and heard in the visions. The symbols and images he saw were things the readers back then understood. These symbols and images were meant to strengthen people's hope that God will ultimately win over Satan and all things evil. This is what John wrote:

This is the revelation that God gave to Jesus Christ. Jesus shows those who serve God what will happen soon. God made it known by sending his angel to his servant John. John gives witness to everything he saw. The things he gives witness to are God's word and what Jesus Christ has said.

Blessed is the one who reads the words of this prophecy. Blessed are those who hear it and think everything it says is important. The time when these things will come true is near.

I, John, am writing this letter.

I am sending it to the seven churches in Asia Minor.

May grace and peace come to you from the One who is, and who was, and who will come. May grace and peace come to you from the seven spirits who are in front of God's throne. May grace and peace come to you from Jesus Christ. What Jesus gives witness to can always be trusted. He was the first to rise from the dead. He rules over the kings of the earth.

Give glory and power to the One who loves us! He has set us free from our sins by pouring out his blood for us. He has made us members of his royal family. He has made us priests who serve his God and Father. Give him glory and power for ever and ever! Amen.

Look! He is coming with the clouds!
    Every eye will see him.
Even those who pierced him will see him.
    All the nations of the earth will be sad
        because of him.
            This will really happen! Amen.

"I am the Alpha and the Omega, the First and the Last," says the Lord God. "I am the One who is, and who was, and who will come. I am the Mighty One."

I, John, am a believer like you. I am a friend who suffers like you. As members of Jesus' royal family, we can put up with anything that happens to us.

I was on the island of Patmos because I taught God's word and what Jesus said. The Holy Spirit took complete control of me on the Lord's Day. I heard a loud voice behind me that sounded like a trumpet. The voice said, "Write on a scroll what you see. Send it to the seven churches in Asia Minor … "

I turned around to see who was speaking to me. When I turned, I saw seven golden lampstands. In the middle of them was someone who looked "like a son of man."

He was dressed in a long robe with a gold strip of cloth around his chest. The hair on his head was white like wool, as white as snow. His eyes were like a blazing fire. His feet were like bronze metal glowing in a furnace. His voice sounded like rushing waters. He held seven stars in his right hand. Out of his mouth came a sharp sword that had two edges. His face was like the sun shining in all of its brightness.

When I saw him, I fell at his feet as if I were dead.

Then he put his right hand on me and said, "Do not be afraid. I am the First and the Last. I am the Living One. I was dead. But look! I am alive for ever and ever! And I hold the keys to Death and Hell.

"So write down what you have seen. Write about what is happening now and what will happen later."

Jesus was showing John all these things so he could tell churches the wonderful things that would happen in the future. This letter would encourage the believers to keep their faith strong and to show people to keep believing in Jesus no matter what, because Jesus would come back to do away with all the evil in the world and reward the people who followed him.

After this I looked, and there in front of me was a door standing open in heaven. I heard the voice I had heard before. It sounded like a trumpet. The voice said, "Come up here. I will show you what must happen after this."

At once the Holy Spirit took complete control of me. There in front of me was a throne in heaven with someone sitting on it. The One who sat there shone like jewels. Around the throne was a rainbow that looked like an emerald.

Twenty-four other thrones surrounded that throne. Twenty-four elders were sitting on them. The elders were dressed in white. They had gold crowns on their heads.

From the throne came flashes of lightning, rumblings and thunder. Seven lamps were blazing in front of the throne. These stand for the seven spirits of God. There was something that looked like a sea of glass in front of the throne. It was as clear as crystal.

In the inner circle, around the throne, were four living creatures. They were covered with eyes, in front and in back. The first creature looked like a lion. The second looked like an ox. The third had a man's face. The fourth looked like a flying eagle. Each of the four living creatures had six wings. Each creature was covered all over with eyes, even under the wings. Day and night, they never stop saying,

"Holy, holy, holy
is the Lord God who rules over all.
He was, and he is, and he will come."

The living creatures give glory, honor and thanks to the One who sits on the throne and who lives for ever and ever. At the same time, the 24 elders fall down and worship the One who sits on the throne and who lives for ever and ever. They lay their crowns in front of the throne. They say,

"You are worthy, our Lord and God!
    You are worthy to receive glory and honor and power.
You are worthy because you created all things.
    They were created and they exist.
    That is the way you planned it."

All creatures in heaven, on earth, under the earth, and on the sea, and all that is in them, were singing. I heard them say,

"May praise and honor for ever and ever
    be given to the One who sits on the throne and to the
        Lamb!
Give them glory and power for ever and ever!"

The four living creatures said, "Amen." And the elders fell down and worshiped.

I saw heaven standing open. There in front of me was a white horse. Its rider is called Faithful and True. When he judges or makes war, he is always fair. His eyes are like blazing fire. On his head are many crowns. A name is written on him that only he knows. He is dressed in a robe dipped in blood. His name is The Word of God.

The armies of heaven were following him, riding on white horses. They were dressed in fine linen, white and clean.

Out of the rider's mouth comes a sharp sword. He will strike down the nations with it. Scripture says, "He will rule them with an iron rod."

The things John saw were meant to show how powerful and mighty God is, not to scare us. When we get to heaven, we'll be very happy and safe there. The best things on earth will be even better than we can imagine.

Jesus is called the Passover lamb because he died on the cross to save us from our sins. John uses this same idea here, calling Jesus the Lamb of God.

Then he carried me away in a vision. The Spirit took me to a huge, high mountain. He showed me Jerusalem, the Holy City. It was coming down out of heaven from God. It shone with the glory of God. It gleamed like a very valuable jewel. It was like a jasper, as clear as crystal.

The city had a huge, high wall with 12 gates. Twelve angels were at the gates, one at each of them. On the gates were written the names of the 12 tribes of Israel. There were three gates on the east and three on the north. There were three gates on the south and three on the west. The wall of the city had 12 foundations. Written on them were the names of the 12 apostles of the Lamb.

The angel who talked with me had a gold measuring rod. He used it to measure the city, its gates and its walls.

The city was laid out like a square. It was as long as it was wide. The angel measured the city with the rod. It was 1,400 miles long. It was as wide and high as it was long.

He measured the wall of the city. It was 200 feet thick. The angel did the measuring as a man would. The wall was made out of jasper. The city was made out of pure gold, as pure as glass.

The 12 gates were made from 12 pearls. Each gate was made out of a single pearl. The main street of the city was made out of pure gold, as clear as glass.

I didn't see a temple in the city. This was because the Lamb and the Lord God who rules over all are its temple. The city does not need the sun or moon to shine on it. God's glory is its light, and the Lamb is its lamp.

The nations will walk by the light of the city. The kings of the world will bring their glory into it. Its gates will never be shut, because there will be no night there. The glory and honor of the nations will be brought into it.

Only what is pure will enter it. No one who fools others or does shameful things will enter it. Only those whose names are written in the Lamb's Book of Life will enter the city.

In this part of the vision, John is saying that the people who followed the Lamb (Jesus) will get to live in this wonderful city someday.

John had more news—Jesus is coming back to earth someday so that all the believers can live with him forever. Here's what he wrote:

[Jesus says,] "Look! I am coming soon! Blessed are those who obey the words of the prophecy in this book."

I, John, am the one who heard and saw these things.

After I had heard and seen them, I fell down to worship at the feet of the angel. He is the one who had been showing me these things.

But he said to me, "Don't do that! I serve God, just as you do. I am God's servant, just like the other prophets and all who obey the words of this book. Worship God!"

Then he told me, "Do not seal up the words of the prophecy in this book. These things are about to happen. Let those who do wrong keep on doing wrong. Let those who are evil continue to be evil. Let those who do what is right keep on doing what is right. And let those who are holy continue to be holy."

"Look! I am coming soon! I bring my rewards with me. I will reward each person for what he has done. I am the Alpha and the Omega. I am the First and the Last. I am the Beginning and the End.

"Blessed are those who wash their robes. They will have

the right to come to the tree of life. They will be allowed to go through the gates into the city.

"I, Jesus, have sent my angel to give you this witness for the churches. I am the Root and the Son of David. I am the bright Morning Star."

The Holy Spirit and the bride say, "Come!" Let those who hear say, "Come!" Anyone who is thirsty should come. Anyone who wants to take the free gift of the water of life should do so.

I am warning everyone who hears the words of the prophecy of this book. If you add anything to them, God will add to you the plagues told about in this book. If you take any words away from this book of prophecy, God will take away from you your share in the tree of life. He will also take away your place in the Holy City. This book tells about these things.

He who gives witness to these things says, "Yes. I am coming soon."

Amen. Come, Lord Jesus!

May the grace of the Lord Jesus be with God's people. Amen.

Discussion Questions

1. Jesus could come back tomorrow, in ten years, or in one hundred years. What can you do to get ready for his return?
2. What do you think heaven will be like?

List of Bible Excerpts

Chapter 1: The Beginning of Life as We Know It

Genesis 1:1–11, 13–31
Genesis 2:1–3, 15–17
Genesis 3:1–23
Genesis 6:5–6, 8–10, 13, 14–22
Genesis 7:1, 17–21, 23–24
Genesis 8:1–5; 15–19, 20
Genesis 9:1–2, 9, 11–13, 16

Chapter 2: God Builds a Nation

Genesis 12:1–5
Hebrews 11:8
Genesis 13:5–6, 14–18
Genesis 15:1–6
Genesis 17:1–8, 15–16
Genesis 21:1–3, 5–7
Hebrews 11:11

Chapter 3: Joseph: From Slave to Deputy Pharaoh

Genesis 37:13–14, 18–28, 31–35
Genesis 39:1–6, 19–23
Genesis 41:8, 14–16, 37–44
Genesis 45:4–8, 13, 25–28
Genesis 46:28–29
Genesis 47:11

Chapter 4: Out of Egypt

Exodus 1:8–11, 22
Exodus 2:1–12
Exodus 3:1–8, 9–12
Exodus 4:10–17
Exodus 7:14–24
Exodus 11:1
Exodus 12:31–32, 40–41
Exodus 13:21–22
Exodus 14:3–6, 8–9, 10–28
Exodus 16:6–7, 9–18

Chapter 5: New Rules

Exodus 20:2–10, 11–17
Exodus 24:3
Exodus 25:1–2, 8–9

Chapter 6: Wandering

Numbers 13:1–3, 18–21, 23, 25–28, 30–33
Numbers 14:1–5, 7–9
Numbers 20:2–12
Deuteronomy 34:10–12

Chapter 7: The Battle Begins

Joshua 1:1–3, 5–7, 10–11
Joshua 2:2–16, 22–23
Joshua 6:10–16, 20, 23–24, 27

Chapter 8: A Few Good Men … and Women

Judges 2:7–8, 10–13
Judges16:4–26, 28, 29, 30
Judges 2:7–8

Chapter 9: The Faith of a Foreign Woman

Ruth 1:6–19
Ruth 2:2–3, 4–23
Ruth 4:13–17

Chapter 10: Messages from God

1 Samuel 1:10–13, 15–18, 20, 25–28
1 Samuel 2:1–2, 21
1 Samuel 3:1–10
1 Samuel 8:1, 3–22
1 Samuel 9:15–21
1 Samuel 10:1–2, 5–7, 9

Chapter 11: From Shepherd to King

1 Samuel 17:1, 2–6, 7, 8, 20–24, 28–35, 37, 40–49
Psalm 59:1–5, 9–10, 16–17

Chapter 12: A King Makes Bad Choices

Psalm 51:1–12
Psalm 32:10–11
1 Chronicles 29:1–6, 9–13, 17–20
Psalm 23:1–6

Chapter 13: The King Who Had It All

1 Kings 3:1–15
1 Kings 4:29–30
Proverbs 1:2–4, 7
Proverbs 3:1–9, 12
Proverbs 20:15, 17
Proverbs 21:23, 30–31
1 Kings 8:22–24, 27–30
2 Chronicles 6:40–42
2 Chronicles 7:1–3
1 Kings 10:1–4, 6–9
1 Kings 11:9–13

Chapter 14: A Kingdom Torn in Two

1 Kings 14:22–23, 26–28
1 Kings 15:11–17, 22–24
1 Kings 16:30–33

Chapter 15: God's Messengers

1 Kings 17:1–6
1 Kings 18:1–2, 17–24, 39–40
1 Kings 19:1–16, 18
2 Kings 2:1–2, 7–15
Amos 3:1–2, 9–11
Amos 4:2, 6, 10, 12
Amos 5:6, 14–15
Amos 9:8

Chapter 16: The Beginning of the End

Isaiah 3:1–5, 8–9, 12–13
Isaiah 14:1–5
Isaiah 49:8–9
Isaiah 53:1–12

Chapter 17: The Kingdoms' Fall

Jeremiah 1:4–10
Jeremiah 2:21–22, 26–28
Jeremiah 5:1
Jeremiah 13:17–19
2 Chronicles 36:15–16, 11–14
2 Kings 25:1–7, 11–12
Lamentations 1:1
Lamentations 2:17
Lamentations 3:21–26
Lamentations 5:1, 15–16, 19–21
Ezekiel 1:1, 4–6, 22–28
Ezekiel 2:1–4, 6–7,
Ezekiel 36:22–28, 33–36

Chapter 18: God Watches Over Daniel

Daniel 6:1–23
Jeremiah 30:2–3, 8, 10–11
Jeremiah 31:23–25
Jeremiah 29:10–14

Chapter 19: The Return Home

Ezra 1:1–7
Ezra 3:10–13, 4:4–5
Ezra 4:24
Haggai 1:2–11
Zechariah 8:2–13, 16–17, 20–22
Ezra 5:13–17
Ezra 6:14, 16–18

Chapter 20: The Queen of Beauty and Courage

Esther 2:10–12, 16, 17–18
Esther 3:1–6, 8, 9, 11, 12
Esther 5:1–8
Esther 7:1–6

Chapter 21: Rebuilding the Walls

Ezra 7:1, 7, 10–11
Nehemiah 1:2–6, 11
Nehemiah 4:4–6, 13–23
Nehemiah 8:1–3, 5–6, 9, 10, 12

Chapter 22: The Birth of the King

John 1:1–5, 9–14, 17–18
Luke 1:26–35, 38, 46–55
Matthew 1:19–24
Luke 2:1, 3–20
Matthew 2:1–3
Luke 2:41–52

Chapter 23: Jesus' Ministry Begins

Matthew 3:1–2, 4–6, 13–17
Matthew 4:1–11
John 1:19–34
Mark 1:31–34, 40–45
Mark 2:1–12
Matthew 4:24–25
Mark 3:9–12, 13–15
Luke 8:1–3

Chapter 24: No Ordinary Man

Mark 4:30–34
Luke 15:1–7
Luke 10:25–37
Matthew 5:2–12
Matthew 6:5–15
Matthew 6:25–34
Mark 4:35–41
Mark 6:30–38, 41–44
Matthew 14:22–33
John 6:66–71

Chapter 25: Jesus, the Son of God

Mark 8:27–30, 34–38
Mark 9:30–32
John 7:11–15, 25–31
John 8:12–14, 31–32
John 11:17–19, 38–48
Mark 10:13–16
John 11:55–57
Mark 11:2–10
Matthew 21:10–11
John 12:27–33, 37, 42–50
Mark 14:1–2
Luke 22:3–6

Chapter 26: The Hour of Darkness

Mark 14:12–17
John 13:21–22, 25–30
Matthew 26:26–28
John 14:1–15
Matthew 26:33–42
Luke 22:43–44
Matthew 26:43–47
John 18:4–10
Luke 22:51, 55–62
John 19:1–7, 16
Matthew 27:32
Luke 23:32–45
Matthew 27:46–49
John 19:30
Matthew 27:51–54
Luke 23:48–49

Chapter 27: The Resurrection

Matthew 28:2–8
John 20:3–10
Luke 24:36–49
John 21:1–6
Matthew 28:16–20

Chapter 28: New Beginnings

Acts 1:2–11
Acts 2:1–6, 23–24, 32–33, 42–47
Acts 8:4–8
Acts 9:1–19
Acts 12:1–18

Chapter 29: Paul's Mission

Acts 16:16–36
1 Thessalonians 1:2–5
1 Thessalonians 4:16–18
1 Thessalonians 5:16–28
1 Thessalonians 3:9–13
1 Corinthians 1:10
1 Corinthians 12:12–18, 27
1 Corinthians 13:1–8
1 Corinthians 15:21–22
1 Corinthians 16:23–24
Galatians 5:22–25
Galatians 6:18

Chapter 30: Paul's Final Days

Acts 20:22–28, 36–38
Acts 22:22–29
Acts 27:1, 9–41
Acts 28:1–10

Chapter 31: Revelation

Revelation 1:1–19
Revelation 4:1–11
Revelation 5:13–14
Revelation 19:11–15
Revelation 21:10–18, 21–27
Revelation 22:7–14, 16–21